TROPICAL FISH IN COLOUR

By
BRAZ WALKER

BLANDFORD PRESS
POOLE   **DORSET**

Photos by Braz Walker and others

INTRODUCTION

The keeping and breeding of tropical aquarium fishes as a hobby, a vocation, an occupation and a profession has assumed enormous proportions in recent years.

It has been said that there is not a biological function found in Nature which is not performed by a living fish. If indeed there are such functions, they are few and obscure. The aquarium is a macrocosm and a microcosm of which the aquarist is in charge, and those biological functions which encompass a universe of constantly unfolding beauty, function, creation and generation are at his disposal. His interest may be completely simple, merely a desire to be exposed to the presence of active, living beauty. Perhaps fulfillment for his desire may consist of a simple container of guppies with their endless action and individually unique variation. On the other hand it may take form in research on, for example, the ability of certain fishes to navigate electrically, sending, receiving and computing information from complicated electrical signals which the creature himself generates.

Our shrinking world has made available to the keeper of fishes an almost unbelievable diversity of fishes, for the remote jungle stream is only hours away, seldom more than days away, in time and distance.

Fishes that fly, fishes that crawl, fishes that hop or slither, fishes that shock, and fishes that sting are available and kept in aquaria. Our wealth perhaps is responsible for some confusion, and this volume has as one of its purposes the combining of lens with printed word to expose the beauty and identity of a select cross-section of some of these, our aquatic contemporaries.

Within these pages you will find mention of such things as pH and hardness of water. The first is simply a method of stating whether water is acid, alkaline, or neither, in which case it would be neutral. Neutral pH is 7.0, acid is any number less than 7.0, and alkaline is any number more than 7.0. In other words pH 6.8 is mildly acid; pH 7.2 is mildly alkaline. A small and inexpensive kit for testing pH is available from most fish dealers.

Hardness of water refers to the dissolved calcium and magnesium salts in water. These are the same salts which affect the ability of soap to make suds. Your local water authority can probably tell you if your water is hard, soft or medium. Kits are available for making hardness tests, and materials for softening excessively hard water can be purchased also.

Most aquarium fishes, especially those which have been popular for many years, have a wide range of tolerance for water conditions, and it is my recommendation to beginners in particular not to attempt altering the chemical makeup of your water unless it is extreme in some way or unless it is specifically indicated for a given species. Simplest terminology was purposely used concerning chemical composition of water; for instance: "Moderately soft, slightly acid water . . ." It is beyond the scope and purpose of this book to go into rigidly technical pursuits and terminology. If a death toll could be taken, it would not be surprising to the author if more fishes have succumbed to having had their water "corrected" than have expired because the tap water was unbearable. It MUST be remembered, however, most city water supplies are treated with chlorine for purification, and this gas is deadly to fishes, especially large carps or minnows such as *Barbus schwanenfeldi*, the tinfoil barb. Fortunately, chlorine will escape from water when it is allowed to stand for 24 hours, or can immediately be rendered harmless by addition of commercially available chlorine removers or sodium thiosulphate at the rate of 1 teaspoon per 25 gallons of freshly drawn water.

FACTS ON FISHES

Scientists use the various characteristics of fishes to classify them. Here are some illustrations of common physical features useful to the aquarist in recognizing tropical fishes, characteristics mentioned from time to time in this book.

IDENTIFING FISH

TETRA

SUNFISH

MODIFIED VENTRALS (GOBY)

PUFFER

CARP

GOURAMI

CATFISH

POECILIID

LOACH

6

The ADIPOSE FIN or "fat fin" is usually fleshy, often small, and located between the dorsal and caudal fins on the back of the fish. Ordinarily it has no rays, although there are exceptions. Typical fishes usually having adipose fins are tetras and catfishes.

The DORSAL FIN is located on the upper back of most fishes. It may be large, small or even absent, and can consist of soft rays, spiny rays or both.

The CAUDAL FIN is simply the tail. Schooling fishes such as tetras or carps (minnows) often have forked caudals, while others, such as cichlids or sunfishes, may have rather squared caudals, relying more on strength than speed.

The PECTORAL FINS are the breast fins. They are paired. The VENTRAL or PELVIC FINS, also paired, are on the lower or pelvic side, a varying distance in front of the VENT. The vent includes the ANUS, and the GENITAL PAPILLA, from which come eggs or living young in the female and milt (sperm) in the male.

The ANAL FIN is just behind the vent, and often is quite similar to the dorsal, except it is located on the underside. Dorsal, anal and caudal fins are called VERTICAL FINS.

Pectoral and ventral fins are called PAIRED FINS. Fins are sometimes MODIFIED for special uses. Like the dorsal fin, spines as well as soft rays may be present in pectorals, ventrals or anal fins.

Some fishes have SCALES, others do not. Some

have smooth skin and are called NAKED. Others have bony armour plates called SCUTES and still others have prickly spines called DERMAL SPINES.

BARBELS are tactile organs which, because of our human tendency to classify everything in relationship to ourselves, look like, and in fact are called by many "whiskers". Actually their usual purpose is to taste, smell and touch.

TETRAS and their relatives usually swim in schools, have adipose fins, forked caudals, scales and no barbels.

BARBS and other carps or minnows usually have soft fin rays, forked caudals, scales, often small barbels and often swim in schools. They have no adipose.

LOACHES are similar to carps in many ways. They have small barbels many times, often are long and slender, and must often keep swimming in order to stay up in the water. There is usually a prickly, sharp bony spine located in a groove beneath the eye which can be erected for protection almost like a switchblade.

CATFISHES usually have adipose fins, barbels and may be naked or with bony scutes which serve as armour.

KILLIES are usually small, often rather pike-shaped, and are characterized by the males often being quite brightly hued while the females usually are rather drab or plain.

POECILIIDS, often called "livebearers" because

their babies are born alive and fully developed, are characterized by the anal fin of the male which is modified into a breeding organ or gonopodium and the dark spot at the vent of pregnant females of most species.

RAINBOW FISHES are recognized by possessing two dorsal fins and slender, streamlined bodies.

SUNFISHES, CICHLIDS and other perch-like fishes are often recognized by their rather stocky bodies which are scaled, and by having both hard and soft fin rays.

GOBIES sometimes have the ventral fins fused into a suction-disc, allowing them to assume odd positions attached to the tank glass or plant leaves.

ANABANTIDS or bubble-nest builders, such as gouramies, are rather perch-like, often have the ventral fins elongated and modified into "feelers" and are capable of breathing atmospheric air.

PUFFERS are usually rather egg-shaped when deflated, but can inflate themselves into globe-shaped forms with either air or water. Inflation sometimes produces numerous sharp dermal spines, making some puffers almost like aquatic porcupines.

Obviously, this is a completely non-technical approach to physical characteristics. It is intended briefly to help familiarize the unfamiliar with a few basic terms and features which will be useful in this book and others dealing with the piscine members of the aquatic kingdom.

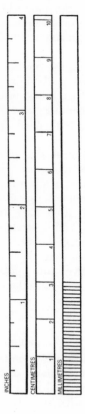

LINEAR CONVERSIONS

The linear system has been used to specify lengths and dimensions in this book. Conversions into the metric scale are given below.

in.	cm.	in.	cm.	in.	cm.
¼	0.6	2½	6.3	7	17.8
½	1.3	3	7.6	8	20.3
1	2.5	4	10.2	9	22.9
1½	3.8	5	12.7	10	25.4
2	5.1	6	15.2	12	30.5

CONTENTS

11

ORDER: *Osteoglossiformes*   FAMILY: *Pantodontidae*
SCIENTIFIC NAME: *Pantodon buchholzi* Peters.
POPULAR NAME: **Butterfly Fish; Chisel Jaw.**
RANGE: Tropical West Africa; Congo: Niger.
HABITAT: Heavily vegetated, standing or slow-moving, often stagnant waters. Ditches; forest ponds.
DESCRIPTION: Body brownish grey or green, moderately robust, with variable dark markings; mouth large, directed upward. Pectorals very large, wing-like; ventrals with extremely long fin-rays. *Male:* Anal fin notched, middle rays forming a tube-like extension. *Female:* Anal plain
LENGTH: 5 inches.
CARE: A well covered aquarium is essential, since this is a "flying fish" capable of leaping and gliding good distances. Planting is desirable, although plenty of surface swimming room should be provided. Not to be kept with fishes inclined toward fin-nipping such as tiger barbs, or surface fishes small enough to be swallowed. Best kept with butterflies only, although community situations can be successful with careful planning. Temp. 75-80°F.—24-27°C. Water moderately soft and acid, although most have considerable toleration for hardness and pH if not extreme.
FEEDING: Preferably live insects, such as meal worms
BREEDING: Difficult. Floating eggs expelled at surface. Young quite difficult to raise

12

Butterfly Fish; Chisel Jaw

ORDER: *Cypriniformes*   FAMILY: *Characidae*
SCIENTIFIC NAME: *Alestes longipinnis* (Günther).
POPULAR NAME: **Longfin Tetra; African Longfin.**
RANGE: West Africa; Congo to Sierra Leone.
HABITAT: Rivers and streams.
DESCRIPTION: Eye bright red, fins clear, body silvery olive green or olive yellow, black longitudinal caudal band with shining golden orange spot above. Mature male with extremely long dorsal.
LENGTH: 5 inches, usually considerably less.
CARE: Roomy, well-lit aquarium with plenty of free-swimming space. Must be covered. No tender plants. Tankmates of similar size and should not be delicate. Aeration preferred, clear water, pH 6.5-7.2, Temp. 70-80°F.—21-27°C.
FEEDING: Live, frozen, freeze-dried tubifex, brine shrimp, insect larvae, high quality dry food, etc.
BREEDING: Typical characid egg-scatterer. Difficult. Soft water required. First food: babies can eat tiny brine shrimp when free-swimming, although infusoria may be used. Breeding temperature 78-80°F.—26-27°C.

Longfin Tetra; African Longfin

Arnold's Tetra

ORDER: *Cypriniformes*   FAMILY: *Characidae*
SCIENTIFIC NAME: *Arnoldichthys spilopterus* (Boulenger).
POPULAR NAME: **Arnold's Tetra.**
RANGE: West Africa; Lagos to Niger.
HABITAT: Rivers, streams.
DESCRIPTION: *Male:* Beautiful coloration, very large scales, eye bright red, upper side brownish, sides iridescent green to blue-green, dark longitudinal band from operculum through anal, accompanied by rainbow-hued lighter band, belly golden to reddish gold. *Female:* Less spectacular, slightly convex anal.
LENGTH: $2\frac{1}{2}$ inches.
CARE: Roomy aquarium with plenty of free-swimming space, not too thickly planted. Best kept with other small, peaceful characids and minnows, etc. Soft, slightly acid water preferred. Aeration, clear water and dark bottom desirable. Not too bright lighting. Temp. 75-85°F.—24-29°C.
FEEDING: Accepts most foods. Live food or equivalent needed often, highest quality flake foods.
BREEDING: Seldom if ever bred in captivity.

Cardinal Tetra

ORDER: *Cypriniformes*   FAMILY: *Characidae*

SCIENTIFIC NAME: *Cheirodon axelrodi* Schultz.

POPULAR NAME: **Cardinal Tetra.**

RANGE: Upper Rio Negro, South America.

HABITAT: Forest pools.

DESCRIPTION: Brilliant neon blue-green longitudinal band from below adipose through eye; fins clear; throat and belly brilliant red to caudal root. Slightly larger than Neon Tetra (*H. innesi*). *Male:* Smaller, slimmer. *Female:* Plumper, more robust.

LENGTH: 2 inches.

CARE: Keep in schools or shoals of several fish, not too bright lighting, accompanied by other small and peaceful fishes such as small barbs, tetras and rasboras. Aeration beneficial. Water should be clear, neutral to somewhat acid, moderately soft to soft. Temp. 70-80°F.—21-27°C. Planting appreciated.

FEEDING: Easily fed. Small live foods, frozen or freeze-dried, as well as high quality dried food. Also scraped beef heart.

BREEDING: Considered "problem fish". Scrupulously clean, preferably all-glass aquaria of 3-5 gallons, soft, crystal clear and acid (pH 6.0-6.5) water. Temp. 78-80°F.—26-27°C. Condition pair on live or frozen food. Do not feed in breeding aquarium. Plants should be cleaned, sterilized, whether artificial or natural such as *Myriophyllum*. Remove parents after spawning, darken aquarium. First food, infusoria.

ORDER: *Cypriniformes*   FAMILY: *Characidae*
SCIENTIFIC NAME: *Colossoma nigripinne* (Cope).
POPULAR NAME: **Black-finned Pacu.**
RANGE: Guyana, Amazon region.
DESCRIPTION: Caudal, anal, pectorals and ventrals a flat black. Lower half deep black from approximately the lateral line downward, demarcation of dark and light zones very irregular, but quite abrupt. Upper half leaden with greenish overcast, throat a dirty white. Rayed adipose fin present. Teeth easily visible.
LENGTH: 2 feet or more; usually much less in the aquarium.
CARE: Unexcelled large show fish needing at least 50-gallon aquarium. No plants, since they will be eaten. Does not molest other fishes unless they can be swallowed. Keep with other large fishes of gentle disposition. Water conditions widely tolerable. Temp. 70-82°F.–21-28°C. Aeration beneficial, high speed filtration almost essential for this endlessly hungry species.
FEEDING: Almost anything, as long as there is plenty of it. Boiled oatmeal particularly good. Canned or dried dog food, depending on brand, excellent. Some cloud water less than others. Alfalfa rabbit food pellets also excellent for this vegetarian. Economically impractical to sustain on commercial fish foods. Celery tops also appreciated.
BREEDING: Impractical.

Black-finned Pacu

Black Tetra; Butterfly Tetra

ORDER: *Cypriniformes* FAMILY: *Characidae*
SCIENTIFIC NAME: *Gymnocorymbus ternetzi* (Boulenger).
POPULAR NAME: **Black Tetra; Butterfly Tetra; Petti-
coat Tetra; Blackamoor.**
RANGE: Paraguay; Brazil, Mato Grosso.
DESCRIPTION: Dorsal and anal large, very black in
young fish; latter half of body also deep black,
lessening with increasing age and size. Black streak
through eye; belly silver-white. Adipose fin black
in young, black-edged or dark-edged in older

specimens. *Male:* Smaller; much more slender; usually darker. *Female:* Larger, more robust. More silvery in belly region, especially when ripe.

LENGTH: 2½-3 inches.

CARE: Roomy, moderately to well-planted aquarium with other medium-sized, active fishes. Schooling fish; best kept in groups. Six or eight healthy young Black Tetras are a striking sight, contrasting with and complementing almost any species. Water around neutral and not too hard; not critical at all. Aeration beneficial. Breeders can be conditioned in community aquarium and simply removed to separate aquarium for spawning.

FEEDING: All fish foods eaten enthusiastically. Live, frozen and freeze-dried foods especially good. Fine ground or blended beef heart good conditioner.

BREEDING: Not difficult; good beginner's tetra. Procedure for most non-problem tetras as follows: Temp. 80-82°F.—27-28°C. Bare aquarium except for clean natural or artificial spawning plants. Freshly drawn water aged a day or two; moderately soft to soft; neutral to somewhat acid (pH 7.0-6.4). A bunch of nylon yarn is good spawning "plant" since it can be sterilized in hot water. A false bottom of plastic hardware cloth or a double layer of marbles allows eggs to fall out of parent's reach. One or two plump females and two or three males can be taken from community aquarium for spawning. Chasing, butting, etc., precedes spawning and continues through the act. Spawning may be almost immediate or may not begin for 2-4 days. Do not feed breeders. If spawning does not occur in 4 days, remove and recondition breeders. Aeration is a stimulant to spawning. When one or more females noticeably slimmer, remove breeders. Feed free-swimming babies infusoria or commercial substitute, new-hatched shrimp.

ORDER: *Cypriniformes*   FAMILY: *Characidae*
SCIENTIFIC NAME: *Hemigrammus pulcher* Ladiges.
POPULAR NAME: **Pretty Tetra.**
RANGE: Middle Amazon.
DESCRIPTION: Body greyish-tan, back slightly darker, belly whitish. Upper eye gleaming red; elongated black blotch on caudal peduncle, above which is gleaming copper spot. Shoulder spot, adipose fin present. *Male:* More slender. *Female:* Stockier; more robust.
LENGTH: $1\frac{1}{2}$-2 inches.
CARE: Excellent in well-planted, spacious community of other small, active and peaceful fishes. Best kept in schools. Eye and copper tail-spot give "head and tail-light" effect as *H. ocellifer.* Water neutral to somewhat acid, not too hard. Temperature 75-82°F.—24-28°C.
FEEDING: All small live, frozen or freeze-dried food. High quality flake and dried foods, finely ground beef heart.

Pretty Tetra

BREEDING: Not easy. Well-conditioned pairs placed in thoroughly clean 5-10 gallon aquarium containing only water and sterilized spawning plants (real or artificial) at 80-82°F.–27-28°C. will sometimes spawn. Leave up to 4-5 days. Do not feed. Water soft, slightly acid. If spawning does not occur, remove, recondition, try again. More than one pair sometimes more successful than single pair. Remove after spawning.

ORDER: *Cypriniformes* FAMILY: *Characidae*
SCIENTIFIC NAME: *Hemigrammus rhodostomus* Ahl.
POPULAR NAME: **Rummy-nose Tetra; Red-nosed Tetra.**
RANGE: Lower Amazon.
DESCRIPTION: Outstanding. A beautiful, striking fish with glowing red "nose"; black and white striped tail. Eye red. Body variable with conditions from transluscent grey-green to brownish upper side with white belly. Fins clear with exception of caudal (tail). Adipose.
LENGTH: 2 inches.
CARE: Excellent schooling community fish to accompany other small, active and peaceful fishes. Temp. over 75°F.—24°C. and well-planted, roomy aquarium promote appearance. Soft, reasonably acid to neutral water. Aeration beneficial.
FEEDING: Most foods. Good dried or flake foods, preferably sinking; freeze-dried or frozen foods, all live foods of suitable size.
BREEDING: Rather difficult. Sterile aquarium and plants. Temp. 80-82°F.—27-28°C. No sand. Water should be soft, slightly acid. Parents conditioned on live food if possible. Spawning location should be quiet, free of passing traffic or shadows. Remove parents after spawning, as with any other egg-scatterer. Youngsters take infusoria when free-swimming. Babies difficult to raise.

Rummy-nose Tetra

ORDER: *Cypriniformes* FAMILY: *Characidae*
SCIENTIFIC NAME: *Hyphessobrycon callistus serpae* Durbin.

POPULAR NAME: **Serpae Tetra; Red Minor.**

RANGE: Middle Amazon.

DESCRIPTION: Delicate to deep red-orange (variable from one breeder's strain to another), adipose present, a dark shoulder spot running vertically, dorsal mostly black, anal black-edged with white tip. *Male:* More slender. *Female:* More robust, rounder belly.

LENGTH: $1\frac{1}{2}$-2 inches.

CARE: Best kept in schools of several with other small to medium non-aggressive fishes of similar temperament. Planting preferred, with open swimming space. Temp. 70-82°F.—21-28°C. Aeration beneficial, especially at higher temperatures. Reasonably soft, neutral to somewhat acid water preferred. As with most *Hyphessobrycon*s, moderately hard and alkaline (pH 7.2-7.4) water will be tolerated, but best condition, especially for breeding, will not result.

FEEDING: Easily fed almost all standard foods. Finely ground beef heart, frozen, freeze-dried, flake and other dried foods. Live foods generate much enthusiasm.

BREEDING: Clean conditions, clear, soft, slightly acid water. Temp. 80-82°F.—27-28°C. Conditioning of breeders very important. Spawning sometimes easier with several fish than single pair.

Serpae Tetra; Red Minor

Flame Tetra

ORDER: *Cypriniformes* FAMILY: *Characidae*
SCIENTIFIC NAME: *Hyphessobrycon flammeus* Myers.
POPULAR NAME: **Flame Tetra; Red Tetra from Rio.**
RANGE: Brazil, around Rio de Janeiro.
DESCRIPTION: Back grey with greenish tinge, belly grey to whitish; posterior half of fish including dorsal, anal and caudal reddish to brick red. Two "shoulder" blotches, longer vertically. *Male:* Anal dark bordered, more concave. *Female:* Anal profile straighter; body fuller.
LENGTH: $1\frac{1}{2}$-$1\frac{3}{4}$ inches.
CARE: Excellent community inhabitant with other small and peaceful tetras, barbs, etc. Well-planted, moderately to well-lit aquarium. Best kept in schools of several. Water non-critical. Temperature 70-80°F.—21-27°C.
FEEDING: Most fish foods of high quality. Prefers live foods, mosquito larvae, bloodworms, etc. Frozen, freeze-dried, flake or dried foods all taken enthusiastically.
BREEDING: One of the easiest of tetras (characids). Typical characid egg-scatterer, driving energetically and depositing eggs on bunched natural or artificial plants. Water not critical, around neutral and not too hard. Temp. 78-80°F.—26-27°C. Ripe female placed in breeding aquarium one day; two or three energetic males next day. Do not feed in breeding aquarium. Spawn in 1-3 days; remove parents. Eggs hatch in about 24 hours or slightly longer. Babies eat liquid fry food or infusoria when free-swimming; follow with brine shrimp.

Black Neon Tetra

ORDER: *Cypriniformes* FAMILY: *Characidae*
SCIENTIFIC NAME: *Hyphessobrycon herbertaxelrodi*
(Gery).
POPULAR NAME: **Black Neon Tetra, Black Neon.**
RANGE: Brazil; Rio Taquary; Mato Grosso.
DESCRIPTION: Adipose (fat) fin present, fins clear,
eye red in upper half; deep black line from behind
operculum through caudal root; bright, lighter
line of white-gold, yellow or blueish in some
lighting. Back brown. *Male:* Smaller. *Female:* More
robust, belly rounded.
LENGTH: $1\frac{1}{4}$-$1\frac{1}{2}$ inches.
CARE: Peaceful, hardy. Should be kept with other
small, peaceful fishes; keep in small schools or
groups. Soft, neutral to slightly acid or acid water;
aeration desirable. Temperature 72-80°F.—22-
27°C.
FEEDING: Easily fed. Dry food, flake food, small live
or frozen and freeze-dried foods. Sinking food
preferred.
BREEDING: Considered "problem fish". Soft, acid
water and sterile conditions give best results. Condition breeders on live, frozen foods. No feeding in
breeding aquarium. Sterilized artificial or fine-
leaved bunched plants, bare aquarium (no gravel)
for breeding. Typical egg-scattering. Remove
parents after spawning, darken aquarium. Breeding
temp. 80-82°F.—27-28°C. Free-swimming babies
eat infusoria.

ORDER: *Cypriniformes*   FAMILY: *Characidae*
SCIENTIFIC NAME: *Hyphessobrycon innesi* Myers.
POPULAR NAME: **Neon Tetra.**
RANGE: Amazon headwaters.
HABITAT: Forest pools and streams.
DESCRIPTION: Brilliant neon-blue longitudinal band from adipose through eye; belly yellow-white; fins clear; lower rear one-quarter brilliant red through caudal peduncle and beneath neon blue band. *Male:* More slender. *Female:* Plumper, more robust, belly more rounded.
LENGTH: 1½ inches.
CARE: Keep in schools of several with other small, peaceful tetras, rasboras, smallest barbs, etc. Dark bottom, not too bright lighting, plants appreciated. Clear, aerated, moderately soft and neutral to somewhat acid water preferred. Temperature 70-82°F.—21-28°C.
FEEDING: Readily accepts almost any small, meat-based or fish-based food, preferably while sinking. Small live foods, freeze-dried and highest quality dried foods preferred.
BREEDING: Considered "problem fish". All-glass aquaria of 3-5 gallons, spotlessly cleaned. Soft, clear and acid (pH 6.0-6.5) water at 78-80°F.—26-27°C. Artificial or natural bunched plants should be sterilized. Condition on live or frozen foods; no feeding in breeding aquarium. Remove parents after spawning. Darken aquarium. Babies eat infusoria, then brine shrimp when free-swimming.

34

Neon Tetra

Ornate Tetra

ORDER: *Cypriniformes*   FAMILY: *Characidae*

SCIENTIFIC NAME: *Hyphessobrycon ornatus* Ahl.

POPULAR NAME: **Ornate Tetra;** mistakenly "Rosy Tetra", which is another fish, *H. rosaceus.*

RANGE: Guyana, Amazon region.

DESCRIPTION: Adipose present; olive-yellow beneath over-all reddish to dark red; no shoulder spot (as in *H. rosaceus*); dorsal with deep black spot tipped with white; anal and ventrals with white lower anterior rays to tip. *Male:* Dorsal in older males long and flowing, anal longer, more sickle-shaped. *Female:* Plainer in finnage, smaller.

LENGTH: $2\frac{1}{2}$ inches.

CARE: Schooling fish, best kept in groups; excellent show fish in community situation with other medium-sized tetras and barbs, planting, aeration appreciated. Temp. 70-82°F.—21-28°C. clear, moderately soft neutral to somewhat acid water.

FEEDING: Easily fed on high quality dried and flake foods, freeze-dried, frozen and live foods. As with most other tetras, prefers sinking or moving food.

BREEDING: Considered "problem fish". Typical characid egg-scatterer, spawning on natural or artificial plant bunches; sterile conditions, 5-10 gallon aquarium, bare aquarium floor. Egg-eater; remove parents after spawning. Soft, acid water best for spawning. First food: infusoria.

ORDER: *Cypriniformes*   FAMILY: *Characidae*
SCIENTIFIC NAME: *Hyphessobrycon pulchripinnis* Ahl.
POPULAR NAME: **Lemon Tetra.**
RANGE: Amazon Basin.
DESCRIPTION: Moderately deep-bodied, compressed. Adipose present. Transluscent yellowish-green on body. Eye bright red. Anal black-edged, rather long-based, first rays a striking, enamel-like lemon yellow for which fish was popularly named. Dorsal dark-edged. *Male:* Smaller, more slender. Anal more intensely black-edged. *Female:* Somewhat larger when grown; heavier-bodied and fuller.
LENGTH: $1\frac{3}{4}$-2 inches.
CARE: Most satisfactory and attractive schooling fish for mid-lower portion of community aquarium containing other small and peaceful fishes. Should be kept in schools. Well-planted, moderately to brightly lit aquarium. Water around neutral, not too hard; not critical. Temp. 70-80°F.—21-27°C.
FEEDING: Prefers small live or frozen foods. Accepts most fish foods, prefers sinking or moving food.
BREEDING: Will spawn on plants or artificial substitute, such as nylon mops, in clean, aerated 5-gallon aquarium. Trios or more of conditioned, well-fed fish may breed more readily than single pairs. Remove fish after spawning, which may take 2-3 days, during which they should not be fed. Moderately soft, slightly acid or neutral water; temperature 80°F.—27°C. Free-swimming babies eat infusoria, liquid fry food, followed by newly-hatched brine shrimp.

38

Lemon Tetra

ORDER: *Cypriniformes*   FAMILY: *Characidae*

SCIENTIFIC NAME: *Hyphessobrycon rubrostigma* Hoedeman.

POPULAR NAME: **Bleeding Heart Tetra ; Tetra Perez.**

RANGE: Colombia.

DESCRIPTION: A deep-bodied *Hyphessobrycon*, adipose present, delicate reddish-brown. Dorsal white-tipped, with prominent black blotch. Vertical black bar through eye. Striking blood-red spot in middle of side, almost as if heart had been pierced ("bleeding heart"). *Male:* Dorsal in older specimens greatly prolonged, possibly reaching to upper caudal lobe in length; anal also quite prolonged and sickle-shaped. Striking. *Female:* Smaller, shorter finnage and more round-bellied.

LENGTH: 3 inches.

CARE: A lively schooling fish, best kept in groups. Tankmates should be medium-large tetras, barbs, etc., not delicate yet not overly aggressive. Rather dense planting, moderately bright lighting, not-too-bright aquarium floor. Water moderately soft, neutral to somewhat acid. Roomy, aerated aquarium appreciated. Temp. 70-80°F.—21-27°C.

FEEDING: Live, freeze-dried and frozen foods, finely ground beef heart, best flake and dried foods, preferably sinking.

BREEDING: Clean, 10-gallon tank; clear, reasonably soft neutral or slightly acid water. Temp. 80-82°F.—27-28°C. Typical *Hyphessobrycon* egg-scatterer (see *H. ornatus*).

Bleeding Heart Tetra

ORDER: *Cypriniformes*　　　FAMILY: *Characidae*
SCIENTIFIC NAME: *Megalamphodus sweglesi* (Gery).
POPULAR NAME: **Red Phantom Tetra; Swegles' Tetra.**
RANGE: Colombia; Amazon.
DESCRIPTION: Reddish brown fins, body transluscent reddish brown; large black shoulder spot; adipose present, dorsal with dark blotch which at times may be more or less obscure. *Male:* Mature males have prolonged dorsal and anal fins. *Female:* Usually slightly larger, dorsal more rounded, more robust.
LENGTH: $1\frac{1}{2}$ inches or slightly more.
CARE: Schooling fish, best kept in groups. Hardy and peaceful, good in community situation with other fishes similar in size and temperament. Moderately soft, neutral to somewhat acid water preferred; plants appreciated. Lively. Temp. 72-82°F.—22-28°C.
FEEDING: Accepts almost all standard fare, prefers sinking or moving foods. Mosquito larvae, bloodworms, etc., taken with much enthusiasm. This is generally true of small and medium characids. Frozen, freeze-dried and flake or dried foods.
BREEDING: Rather difficult, apparently depending greatly on water quality and cleanliness. Breeding temp. 80-82°F.—27-28°C. Standard procedure for the more difficult of the *Hyphessobrycon* species, which are rather similar.

42

Red Phantom Tetra; Swegles' Tetra

Congo Tetra

ORDER: *Cypriniformes*   FAMILY: *Characidae*
SCIENTIFIC NAME: *Micralestes interruptus* Boulenger.
Also known as *Phennacogrammus interruptus*.
POPULAR NAME: **Congo Tetra.**
RANGE: Congo Basin; Stanley Pool.
DESCRIPTION: Body compressed and elongate;
scales rather large. *Male:* Middle caudal rays quite
extended, increasing with age and size; dorsal
extended, often reaching caudal. Rainbow-hued

by reflected light; breathtakingly beautiful in fine specimens. Fins rather steel-grey, sometimes pink or reddish. Anal, caudal light-edged. Adipose fin present. *Female:* Smaller, less handsome. Fins not extended.

LENGTH: 5 inches; usually less.

CARE: Large aquarium, well-planted but with plenty of free-swimming room. Best kept in schools. Good community fish with other active, peaceful and large fishes. Exclude fin-nippers. Soft, slightly acid to acid water is best, especially for prospective breeders, although some gorgeous specimens have been raised within the author's knowledge in moderately soft, slightly alkaline water. A rather touchy species, worth every bit of effort extended in their behalf.

FEEDING: Live food preferred, especially insects. Brine shrimp (frozen), chopped earthworms, beef heart.

BREEDING: Non-adhesive, large eggs laid during hard driving. Sunlight seems to stimulate spawning. Not frequently spawned. Breeding temperature 78-80°F.—26-27°C.

ORDER: *Cypriniformes* FAMILY: *Characidae*
SCIENTIFIC NAME: *Myloplus rubripinnis* (Müller & Troschel).
POPULAR NAME: **Red Hook; Red Hook "Metynnis".**
RANGE: Guyana, Amazon region.
DESCRIPTION: Silvery, disc-shaped, extremely long, sickle-shaped anal. Anal bright red (*rubripinnis* = red fin), edged with black. Adipose present, small and rounded (not "squared" at corners).
LENGTH: 4 to 6 inches, often less.
CARE: Excellent show fish kept with *Metynnis*, *Mylossoma* and other vegetarian, medium-sized members of the sub-family *Serrasalminae*. No plants, since they will be eaten. If possible should be kept in groups or at least in the presence of other "silver dollar" type fishes.
FEEDING: Omnivorous. All high quality foods accepted with enthusiasm. Food should not be too small. Flake or pellet foods, ground beef heart, frozen brine shrimp. Small red worms are excellent. Vegetation in the form of algae, alfalfa, celery or carrot tops should be used frequently. Boiled oatmeal (rolled oats) and cooked spinach are also good.
BREEDING: Unlikely. Soft, moderately acid water at 80-82°F.—27-28°C. desirable. Roomy aquarium. Similar species drive energetically in pairs, male pressing female against spawning medium as eggs are expelled.

Red Hook

Emperor Tetra

ORDER: *Cypriniformes*   FAMILY: *Characidae*
SCIENTIFIC NAME: *Nematobrycon palmeri* Eigenmann.
POPULAR NAME: **Emperor Tetra.**
RANGE: Colombia.
HABITAT: Forest streams.
DESCRIPTION: Back shining steel blue-grey, with golden overtones in some lighting. Wide black streak from mouth to caudal root on lower half of body. Eye neon blue to blue green. *Male:* Caudal

forked, prolonged into three magnificent filaments in older fish; dorsal also with front ray produced into filament. *Female:* Caudal three-pronged, not extended as in male. All fins, especially anal (which in both sexes is outlined in dark and light edge), smaller, less handsome than male. Young fish quite similar.

LENGTH: 2-2½ inches.

CARE: Excellent community fish with other tetras, small minnows such as danios, barbs, etc. Best kept in small schools in moderately well-lighted and well-planted aquarium. Water not too hard, around neutral or slightly acid, not critical. Temperature 70-80°F.—21-27°C.

FEEDING: Accepts all high quality foods. Prefers live and frozen foods, but also relishes finely ground beef heart and flake food.

BREEDING: Spawns on bunched natural or artificial plants. Clean 5-7 gallon aquarium sufficient; water moderately soft; temp. about 80°F.—27°C. Older fish spawn rather readily if separated a few days and fed quantities of live food. Babies can take tiniest brine shrimp when free-swimming.

ORDER: *Cypriniformes*   FAMILY: *Characidae*
SCIENTIFIC NAME: *Pristella riddlei* (Meek).
POPULAR NAME: **Pristella Tetra; X-ray Fish.**
RANGE: Northern South America; Guyana, lower Amazon.

HABITAT: Both standing and flowing water.

DESCRIPTION: Body very slight olive-yellow to olive-greyish; rather transluscent to semi-transparent. Over-all / silvery. Black shoulder spot. Dorsal and anal white-tipped, with black blotches edged by yellowish. Caudal pinkish to reddish. *Male:* More slender. *Female:* More robust; abdomen more rounded.

LENGTH: 2 inches. Fully grown males slightly less.

CARE: A schooling fish, best kept in groups in company of other small and mild-mannered tetras and minnows. Well-planted aquarium with clear water; water uncritical as to pH and hardness if not extreme in one aspect or another. Temp. 72-80°F.—22-27°C. A charming contrast to gaudier tank-mates, and a good beginner's fish with great longevity, considering small size.

FEEDING: Live, frozen or freeze-dried as well as prepared foods of most types. Likes to strike at sinking (moving) food.

BREEDING: Not extremely difficult, but requiring certain skills or experience. Clear, fresh (aged for chlorine escape) water, moderately soft and neutral or slightly acid. Bare aquarium, clean artificial or natural spawning plants Apparently some pairs are incompatible. By using several fish, this can

Pristella Tetra; X-ray Fish

sometimes be overcome. Remove after spawning. Babies hatch in about one day, swim freely in additional day or two. At this time the little glass-like slivers must be fed infusoria, a commercial liquid-type fry food or super-fine, highest quality dried food. The latter is best mixed with a small amount of water from the aquarium and shaken to disperse it and sink it, then added to aquarium. Some aquarists feed tiniest newly hatched brine shrimp as first food. Those that accept this relatively large fare grow rapidly, but not all do so and this can result in some early losses Spawns may be sizeable, 200-400 babies possibly resulting.

COMMENT: This Pristella Tetra's subtlety is perhaps a part of its charm.

ORDER: *Cypriniformes*   FAMILY: *Characidae*

SCIENTIFIC NAME: *Serrasalmus natteri* (Kner).

POPULAR NAME: **Red-breasted Piranha.**

RANGE: Amazon region.

HABITAT: Flowing streams and reasonably calm stretches.

DESCRIPTION: Much compressed, almost disc-shaped body. Caudal dark bordered, breast deep silver-pink to red. Adipose non-rayed; small. Back darkish grey-brown to olive grey. Lower jaw somewhat projected; teeth visible. Back and sides flecked with dark and also rather glittering gold to gold-olive flecks. CAUTION: Capable of biting viciously when handled.

LENGTH: 6-10 inches in aquarium depending on care.

CARE: Best kept singly as show fish. Roomy aquarium; may be planted with sturdiest plants which may or may not be left intact. Darkish bottom, aquarium location away from passing shadows. Water conditions non-critical. Temp. 70-80°F.—21-27°C. Aeration and filtration recommended. Lighting not too bright. A rather nervous fish, especially if overcrowded or frequently moved, or in areas of traffic.

FEEDING: Carnivorous and piscivorous. Small,

Red-breasted Piranha

unwanted fishes, pieces of meat or fish, preferably rinsed to remove excessive juices, earthworms and blocks of freeze-dried foods. Small piranhas fond of pellet-type food.

BREEDING: Unlikely in home aquarium. Other *Serrasalmus* species have occasionally spawned in public aquaria.

COMMENT: This is an excellent, handsome show fish in addition to its curiosity value as one of the infamous "bloodthirsty" piranhas or pirayas, which have upon occasion turned the tables on man, the great piscivore, and made a meal of *him*! Not dangerous if sensibly and reasonably handled.

Boehlke's Penguin Fish

ORDER: *Cypriniformes*   FAMILY: *Characidae*

SCIENTIFIC NAME: *Thayeria boehlkei* Weitzman.

POPULAR NAME: **Boehlke's Penguin Fish.**

RANGE: Amazon region.

DESCRIPTION: Adipose present; black lateral band from behind upper operculum through the somewhat elongated lower caudal lobe. Bronze-green to silver-green on dorsal or upper side, yellowish or silver-blue or green below. *Male:* Slightly smaller and more slender. *Female:* Slightly more rounded ventrally (fuller).

LENGTH: 2½-3 inches.

CARE: Peaceful and hardy; very active. Excellent, striking fish when kept in schools with similar-sized fishes in roomy community aquarium. Keep covered. Temp. 72-82°F.—22-28°C., water moderrately soft and neutral to somewhat acid.

FEEDING: High quality dried or flake foods, frozen and freeze-dried as well as live foods, especially mosquito larvae. More readily takes to surface-feeding than most other small and medium characids because of its normal "tail-standing" swimming attitude.

BREEDING: Clean, preferably sterilized 5-7 (or larger) gallon aquarium. Soft, slightly acid water, artificial or bunched fine-leaved spawning plants (sterilized). Temp. 80-82°F.—27-28°C. Scatters eggs characid-style. Large spawns, up to 1,000 eggs.

ORDER: *Cypriniformes*   FAMILY: *Gasteropelecidae*
SCIENTIFIC NAME: *Gasteropelecus sternicla* (Linnaeus).
POPULAR NAME: **Silver Hatchet Fish.**
RANGE: Guyana, Amazon region.
DESCRIPTION: Body silver with dark stripe from
caudal root to opercular opening, massive pectoral
fins. Breast extremely deep in profile (*Gasteropelecus*
= hatchet belly), wedge-shaped from front. Fins
clear, dorsal far back. Adipose fin present, small.
LENGTH: 2½-3 inches.
CARE: Long-lived, hardy. A "freshwater flying
fish"; MUST be kept covered. Roomy aquarium
best. Good community aquarium occupant with
similar-sized, non-aggressive fishes. Occupies upper-
most level, which should not be excessive with
floating vegetation. Temp. 72-82°F.—22-28°C.
FEEDING: Small, floating live food such as mosquito larvae, *Drosophila*. Best flake and dried foods,
freeze-dried (loose pack preferred) brine shrimp
very good.
BREEDING: Rarely, if ever. Other gasteropelecids
reportedly spawn in clumps of plants near surface
or in the root-systems of surface plants.

Silver Hatchet Fish

ORDER: *Cypriniformes*   FAMILY: *Anostomidae*
SCIENTIFIC NAME: *Leporinus nigrotaeniatus* (Schomburgk).

POPULAR NAME: **Half-lined Leporinus.**

RANGE: Guyana, Amazon region.

DESCRIPTION: Cigar- or torpedo-shaped body, forked caudal, adipose present, other fins clear. Body grey-brown, darker above. Deep black line from caudal to mid-side, halting abruptly. No apparent sex distinctions.

LENGTH: 6 inches in aquarium.

CARE: Excellent jumper; keep covered. Large aquarium with other sturdy fishes, such as other anostomids, cichlids, etc. Only strong-leaved plants are suitable; others will be nipped and nibbled to pieces. Fine show fish for largest aquariums, but rather sneakily aggressive. Nips fins of slow-moving fishes.

FEEDING: Heavy feeder; at least partially vegetarian. Boiled oatmeal (rolled oats) and oatmeal-based preparations excellent. Alfalfa rabbit food pellets, celery tops, cooked spinach appreciated. All fish foods of suitable size.

BREEDING: Impractical.

Half-lined Leporinus

ORDER: *Cypriniformes*   FAMILY: *Chilodóntidae*
SCIENTIFIC NAME: *Chilodus punctatus* Müller & Troschel.

POPULAR NAME: **Headstander; Spotted Headstander.**

RANGE: Guyana; middle and upper Amazon region.

DESCRIPTION: Moderately elongated, missile-shaped body, strongly tapered forward to "point"; mouth small, adipose fin present; large scales. Body grey-brown, back darker, belly and throat whitish. Fins clear except dorsal, which is spotted and dark-tipped. Dark lateral band; alternate dark and light scales give "checkered" appearance. Swims with head downward at approximately 45° angle.

LENGTH: 3½ inches.

CARE: Large aquarium, well-planted, providing not only ample room for swimming free, but retreats such as plant thickets. Temp. 72-82°F.— 22-28°C. Aeration helpful. Good community fish with smaller fishes, which will not be molested (within reason).

FEEDING: Small live foods, algae or other vegetation, such as alfalfa or cooked spinach. Highest quality dried foods or flake foods may be accepted. Food must sink because of head-down feeding position. May nibble tender plants. Some specimens appear to feed, yet grow emaciated in company of aggressive fishes.

BREEDING: Very difficult. Soft, acid water, large aquarium. Spawns on plants, eats eggs if not removed. Temp. 80-82°F.—27-28°C. Condition on live food.

Spotted Headstander

ORDER: *Cypriniformes*   FAMILY: *Distichodontidae*

SCIENTIFIC NAME: *Distichodus sexfasciatus* Boulenger.

POPULAR NAME: **Six-banded Distichodus.**

RANGE: Congo Basin.

DESCRIPTION: Strikingly beautiful. Similar to *D. lusosso* which has a longer, more narrow snout. Reddish yellow to red-brown; about six dark blue to black vertical bands; fins red except adipose which is dark.

LENGTH: Up to 10 inches.

CARE: Aggressive. Should be kept in large aquaria with large fishes able to defend themselves. Eats plants. Distichodontids and the closely related citharinids are excellent jumpers and must be covered. Water not excessively hard, near neutral to acid in pH. Temperature 72-82°F.—22-28°C.

FEEDING: Beef heart, frozen, freeze-dried and live foods. Dried and flake foods in larger grades; also boiled oatmeal. Vegetation, such as algae, alfalfa pellets, cooked spinach, celery tops, etc.

BREEDING: Unlikely.

Six-banded Distichodus

Banded Knife Fish

ORDER: *Cypriniformes*   FAMILY: *Gymnotidae*
SCIENTIFIC NAME: *Gymnotus carapo* Linnaeus.
POPULAR NAME: **Banded Knife Fish.**
RANGE: Guatemala southward, Guyana through Amazon; widespread through tropical South America.
HABITAT: Daylight hours in smaller creeks or weeded areas, ranging into larger waterways at darkness.

DESCRIPTION: Knife-shaped; mouth rather large, vent far forward, preceding anal; anal long, rippling, tapered to a point. Rather eel-like; no dorsal, caudal or ventrals. Anal fin provides propulsion. Scales small; eyes rather small and beady. Greyish-tan, sometimes with greenish tinge; dark bars or bands adorning sides vertically, sometimes blending more or less together. Pattern quite variable. Old fish usually darker. A weakly electric fish.

LENGTH: To 2 feet in nature; less in aquarium.

CARE: Easily maintained. Breathes atmospheric air supplementary to gill-breathing; viciously aggressive with own kind and others of like or smaller size. Withstands abuse and overcrowding amazingly, which is no excuse for trying. Retiring places such as plant thickets or roots much appreciated.

FEEDING: Earthworms can be fed whole, providing clean and easy maintenance Also beef heart, frozen shrimp and small fishes. Temperature 70-82°F.—21-28°C.

BREEDING: Impractical; not bred in captivity.

Rosy Barb

ORDER: *Cypriniformes*   FAMILY: *Cyprinidae*
SCIENTIFIC NAME: *Barbus conchonius* (Hamilton-Buchanan).
POPULAR NAME: **Rosy Barb.**
RANGE: India; Bengal; Assam.
HABITAT: Rivers, streams, ditches; moving water.
DESCRIPTION: Typical "barb-shape". Scales quite large and reflective; back olive-green with sides

and belly lighter, somewhat yellowish olive. Conspicuous black spot just above anal on mid-side. *Male:* At breeding time or when older fish are in prime condition, body flushed with rose-red; fins red. Dorsal, anal and ventrals (pelvics) black-tipped. Very beautiful. *Female:* Plain; silvery olive green. More robust, otherwise same as male without rosy flush.

LENGTH: $3\frac{1}{2}$ inches in aquarium; 6 inches in nature.

CARE: Easily maintained, undemanding, popular. Excellent community fish with other lively, medium sized fishes. Best kept in small schools in roomy, well-planted aquarium. Water conditions most undemanding; temperature 65-85°F.—18-30°C.

FEEDING: Omnivorous. All fish foods eaten with gusto. Live foods or meat-based foods for breeder conditioning. Occasional vegetation beneficial.

BREEDING: Good beginner's barb. Well-conditioned pairs or trios spawn readily on bunched plants at 80°F.—27°C. Egg-eater. Floor of breeding aquarium may be covered with marbles to prevent egg-eating. Remove parents after completion of spawning. Liquid fry food or infusoria followed by newly hatched brine shrimp as first foods. Spawns often large.

Black-spot Barb; Long-finned Barb

ORDER: *Cypriniformes*   FAMILY: *Cyprinidae*
SCIENTIFIC NAME: *Barbus filamentosus* (Cuvier &
Valenciennes).
POPULAR NAME: **Black-spot Barb; Long-finned Barb.**
RANGE: South-west India; Ceylon.
HABITAT: Rivers and streams.
DESCRIPTION: Body greenish silver; olive above; a
large black spot just over anal. Fins yellowish to
pink; dorsal dark red to violet in adult male. Young
with dark bars on body; brick-red fins; not dissimi-
lar to young Clown Barbs (*B. everetti*). *Male:* Dorsal
rays greatly elongated. *Female:* More robust.
LENGTH: 5-6 inches, usually less.
CARE: Large, not too thickly planted aquarium
with other similar-sized fishes. Active, will nip fins
of long-finned fishes such as angelfish. Schooling
fish best kept in groups. Aquarium should be
covered. Temp. 72-82°F.—22-28°C. Water not
critical as to hardness and pH. Aeration is beneficial
and, as with all large cyprinids, this fish is particularly susceptible to chlorine poisoning.
FEEDING: Omnivorous. Live food appreciated.
Boiled oatmeal (rolled oats) good. Occasional
vegetable fare desirable.
BREEDING: Large breeding aquarium. Temp. 80-
82°F.—26-28°C. Hard-driving; spawns on clumps
of plants (real or artificial). Prolific. Excellent for
outdoor pond in warm weather. Babies eat
infusoria or substitute.

ORDER: *Cypriniformes*   FAMILY: *Cyprinidae*
SCIENTIFIC NAME: *Barbus oligolepis* (Bleeker).
POPULAR NAME: **Checkerboard Barb; Checker Barb.**
RANGE: Sumatra.
HABITAT: Lakes and streams.
DESCRIPTION: Delicate reddish brown; back darker, with a pearly blueish lustre. Scales large; each with a dark edge and a blue sheen at base, giving the "checkered" effect. *Male:* Vertical fins reddish to brick-red; dark-edged. *Female:* Plainer; fins yellowish, not black-edged. More robust at maturity.
LENGTH: 2 inches.
CARE: Excellent in community with other small, peaceful fishes. Schooling fish, best kept in groups. Planting desirable, but swimming room should be available. Very active. Temp. 72-82°F.—22-28°C. Water not critical as to pH and hardness, although extremes are undesirable.
FEEDING: Omnivorous. Small live foods especially appreciated. Flake foods taken as they sink.
BREEDING: Not difficult. 5-gallon tank can be half-filled with tap water, covered, allowed to stand 24 hours. Breeders spawn on bunched plants usually on morning after being introduced to tank. Aeration sometimes stimulates spawning. Remove after spawning, since parents are ravenous egg-eaters. Babies are very tiny when free-swimming, needing quantities of infusoria, green water or egg-infusion.

Checkerboard Barb

ORDER: *Cypriniformes*   FAMILY: *Cyprinidae*
SCIENTIFIC NAME: *Barbus pentazona* Boulenger.
POPULAR NAME: **Five-banded Barb.**
RANGE: Malay Peninsula; Borneo; Sumatra.
HABITAT: Small streams; clear or somewhat turbid water over sand, gravel or silt bottom.
DESCRIPTION: Compressed; fairly deep-bodied. Body reddish brown to reddish; five distinct blue-black veritcal bars on sides, often a very narrow, indistinct sixth bar at caudal base. Bars sometimes with yellowish edges. Fins dark red at base, lightening progressively toward outer edge. Two pairs of barbels. *Male:* More slender; brighter. *Female:* More robust.
LENGTH: 2 inches.
CARE: Well-planted, moderately well-lit aquarium providing plant thickets for retirement, but plenty of open swimming space. Less inclined to school than *B. tetrazona*, also less active and nippy. Good community fish. Water moderately soft, slightly acid is best.
FEEDING: Omnivorous. Live foods preferred, supplemented by frozen, flake or dried foods. Should have occasional plant material.
BREEDING: Egg-scatterer, spawning on plants. Not easy, although well-conditioned pairs will spawn. Soft, slightly acid water; 80°F.—27°C.

Five-banded Barb

Aeration may help induce spawning. More than
one pair will sometimes prove successful when single
pair refuses. Eats eggs.

Tinfoil Barb ; Schwanenfeld's Barb

ORDER: *Cypriniformes*   FAMILY: *Cyprinidae*

SCIENTIFIC NAME: *Barbus schwanenfeldi* Bleeker.

POPULAR NAME: **Tinfoil Barb; Schwanenfeld's Barb.**

RANGE: Sumatra; Malacca; Borneo; Thailand.

HABITAT: Widely distributed in rivers.

DESCRIPTION: Body bright silver, as if covered with metal foil. Dorsal with black tip. Caudal, dorsal, anal and ventrals bright mercurochrome-red. Red intensifies greatly with increasing age and size. A most striking, well-mannered and active fish for the largest aquaria. Anal, ventrals white-edged in mature.

LENGTH: 12-14 inches in aquarium (by author); probably more in nature.

CARE: Largest aquarium. Best kept in groups. Needs plenty of swimming room. *Very* sensitive to chlorine poisoning, also excess carbon dioxide. Aeration, filtration strongly recommended; should be lively. Best kept in community with other large, relatively peaceful fishes, such as Black-finned Pacu (*C. nigripinne*).

FEEDING: Omnivorous. Beef heart, dog food either dried or canned, cooked oatmeal, alfalfa rabbit food pellets. Small Tinfoil Barbs take any fish food with gusto; larger specimens capable of eating almost unbelievable quantities, making standard fish foods impractical. Dried, high quality dog foods may be pre-soaked for softening or fed dry. (Do NOT use "gravy" type dog food.)

BREEDING: Unknown. Mature at 6-8 inches, according to H. M. Smith.

75

ORDER: *Cypriniformes*   FAMILY: *Cyprinidae*

SCIENTIFIC NAME: *Barbus semifasciolatus* Günther.

POPULAR NAME: **Gold Barb; Shubert's Barb.**

RANGE: South China; Hainan.

HABITAT: Small, grass-grown irrigation reservoirs, ditches of rice fields.

DESCRIPTION: Wild specimens very variable in shade. Gold domestic variety: *Male:* Body bright yellow gold, fins red orange. A black, semi-broken but distinct lateral band often present. *Female:* Larger, much heavier and more robust; at maturity obviously bulging more than male. Lateral band much less distinct. Otherwise similar.

LENGTH: 2-2½ inches.

CARE: Excellent long-lived member for community tank containing other small to medium barbs and tetras of moderate temperament. Should be kept in small groups if possible. Water completely non-critical (within reason); Temp. 68-82°F.—20-28°C. Aeration beneficial.

FEEDING: Omnivorous. Will accept and thrive on any fish food. Heavy feeder for its size.

BREEDING: One of the easiest egg-layers. One or two heavy females placed in breeding aquarium with two or three healthy-looking, slender males at temp. of 80°F.—27°C., preferably with well-aerated water, will almost invariably spawn in 1-3 days, during which time they should not be fed. A layer of marbles or pebbles on floor of breeding container keeps breeders from eating eggs. Remove

Gold Barb ; Shubert's Barb

breeders when one female appears empty of eggs.
Spawns large. First food: liquid fry food.

ORDER: *Cypriniformes*   FAMILY: *Cyprinidae*

SCIENTIFIC NAME: *Barbus tetrazona* (Bleeker).

POPULAR NAME: **Tiger Barb; Sumatra Barb.**

RANGE: Sumatra; Borneo.

DESCRIPTION: Compressed; rather deep-bodied. Silvery tan to olive on back; scales golden-edged, giving over-all golden impression. Four intense black vertical bands. Ventral (pelvic) fins blood red; dorsal black at base, edged blood red. Other fins pinkish to reddish. *Male:* More slender; mouth red when in breeding condition. *Female:* Heavier; more robust. (See photograph: Male upper, female lower).

LENGTH: 2 inches.

CARE: Best kept in groups or schools in well-planted and well-lit, aerated aquarium containing other lively fishes of similar size and temperament. Ceaselessly active, inclined to nip at other fishes apparently for the joy of it. Single individuals more nippy than group-members. Water around neutral, not too hard, not critical. Temp. 72-80°F.—22-27°C.

FEEDING: Omnivorous. Most small *Barbus* species feed on combination of vegetable, insect and other small animal life in nature. Live foods, good quality flake and dried foods, freeze-dried tubifex, etc.

BREEDING: Spawns in typical barb-style on plants such as *Myriophyllum* or artificial substitutes such as bundles of nylon yarn. Active egg-eater.

Tiger Barb; Sumatra Barb

Spawning temperature about 80°F.—27°C. Bare
5-7 gallon aquarium with clear, clean water and
spawning plants is sufficient.

Cherry Barb

ORDER: *Cypriniformes*   FAMILY: *Cyprinidae*
SCIENTIFIC NAME: *Barbus titteya* (Deraniyagala).
POPULAR NAME: **Cherry Barb.**
RANGE: Ceylon.
HABITAT: Shady streams, creeks.
DESCRIPTION: Elongate, not much compressed. Body reddish-brown; a dark, somewhat broken but quite distinct lateral band of brown to black from caudal through eye. A shining lighter band above, golden to greenish. *Male:* Brilliant cherry-red at breeding time, sometimes maintained continuously when kept in groups under proper conditions. *Female:* Larger, heavier and less handsome. Golden brown, fins yellowish.
LENGTH: 2 inches or less.
CARE: Moderately planted aquarium with other small and peaceful fishes. Schooling fish, best kept in groups of several. Temp. 72-82°F.—22-28°C. Water conditions not too critical, should be moderately soft for best condition.
FEEDING: Omnivorous. Prefers sinking food or live food, such as mosquito larvae or daphnia.
BREEDING: Considered difficult by some authorities, but in personal experience one of the easiest barbs. Eggs may be laid a few at a time, going unobserved. These are promptly eaten, and female appears still full. A double layer of marbles on bottom saves eggs, which fall out of reach. If two pairs are placed in breeding tank, they can be removed when one female is noticeably slimmer. Babies quite small.

81

ORDER: *Cypriniformes*   FAMILY: *Cyprinidae*

SCIENTIFIC NAME: *Brachydanio albolineatus* (Blyth).

POPULAR NAME: **Pearl Danio; Gold Danio.**

RANGE: India; Sumatra,

HABITAT: Flowing water.

DESCRIPTION: Body elongate, slender; a pale, rather iridescent blueish pearl-like tone with reddish to gold lateral band from caudal base to above pectorals. Belly lighter, back somewhat darker. 2 pairs of barbels. *Male:* Smaller, more slender. *Female:* Much heavier when mature and ripe.

VARIATIONS: Body over-all golden to flesh tone.

LENGTH: 2 inches.

CARE: Best kept in schools or groups of several. Very lively and active; occupies middle-upper layers; should have plenty of swimming space. Water conditions non-critical. Aeration appreciated. Temp. 70-80°F.—21-27°C. Good community fish with other small, reasonably well mannered fishes.

FEEDING: Omnivorous. Live, frozen, freeze-dried and almost all dried foods quite acceptable.

BREEDING: Easy; good beginner's egg-layer. Place well-rounded female in small, preferably long and shallow aquarium, or in rod trap or other device designed for breeding non-adhesive egg-layers. Next day place two or three lively males with female; spawning should take place on following morning or next thereafter. Morning sunlight stimulates spawning. Spawning consists of lively driving by males, eggs being released and fertilized, sinking to bottom. If rod trap is used (a box with a

Pearl Danio; Gold Danio

false bottom made of closely spaced glass or plastic rods), eggs fall between rods and out of reach of adults, which are avid egg-eaters. Alternate egg-saving methods are heavy layer of bunched plants on bottom or covering bottom with a layer of marbles or large pea-gravel. Breeders can also be placed in a large-meshed net which allows eggs to fall through. Babies, which may number 200 or more from large, heavy females, are easily raised on liquid fry food or infusoria followed by newly hatched shrimp.

Spotted Danio

ORDER: *Cypriniformes* FAMILY: *Cyprinidae*

SCIENTIFIC NAME: *Brachydanio nigrofasciatus* (Day).

POPULAR NAME: **Spotted Danio.**

RANGE: Upper Burma.

HABITAT: Standing and flowing waters, rivers to smallest pools.

DESCRIPTION: Body rather long and slender; brown to olive-brown or light brown on back, belly yellowish white. Sides with dark blue-black stripes above and below a golden lateral band through middle caudal rays; a broken band of dark spots below. *Male:* More slender, usually slightly smaller. *Female:* Belly more rounded; more robust.

LENGTH: $1\frac{1}{2}$ inches.

CARE: Excellent, active and lively community fish. Best kept in schools in company of other small and lively but inoffensive fishes. Well-lit, well-planted aquarium with plenty of swimming room in upper and middle portions. Temp. 72-80°F.—22-27°C. Water composition not critical.

FEEDING: Omnivorous. Live foods, freeze-dried or frozen foods, flake or dried foods of almost all kinds, preferably floating or slowly sinking.

BREEDING: More difficult than *B. rerio* or *B. albolineatus.* Well-conditioned female should be separated from males for few days in breeding tank. Two or three males then introduced. Rod trap or other egg-saving device may be used, adults removed after spawning. Babies not difficult to raise; feed liquid fry food or infusoria followed by brine shrimp.

ORDER: *Cypriniformes* FAMILY: *Cyprinidae*
SCIENTIFIC NAME: *Brachydanio rerio* (Hamilton-Buchanan).

POPULAR NAME: **Zebra Danio; Zebra Fish.**

RANGE: Bengal; eastern India.

HABITAT: Ponds and streams, other still and moving water.

DESCRIPTION: Body rather long and slender; caudal slightly forked. Body and fins silvery to yellow-white, with four steel-blue lines on sides, three of which extend onto caudal. Anal with three steel-blue bands; dorsal edged in steel-blue or black. Striking in contrast. *Male:* Smaller, more slender; sometimes slightly darker in tone. *Female:* More robust; belly obviously more rounded.

LENGTH: 2 inches.

CARE: Excellent, hardy and lively community fish. Good beginner's fish for both keeping and breeding. Well-lit, well-planted aquarium providing good middle and upper level swimming room. Keep in schools with other small, lively fishes. Water make-up most uncritical. Temp. 65-80°F.—18-27°C. Keep well covered.

FEEDING: Accepts all fish foods enthusiastically. Live food best for conditioning breeders.

BREEDING: One of the easiest egg-layers. Ripe female placed with two or three lively and slender males in 2-5 gallon aquarium with bottom covered by marbles or pebbles will spawn almost invariably.

Zebra Danio

Temp. about 78-80°F.—26-27°C. Place aquarium to receive some early, bright daylight. Aeration stimulates breeders.

ORDER: *Cypriniformes* FAMILY: *Cyprinidae*
SCIENTIFIC NAME: *Danio malabaricus* (Jerdon).
POPULAR NAME: **Giant Danio.**
RANGE: Western India; Ceylon.
HABITAT: Clear flowing water.
DESCRIPTION: Body rather elongate, compressed. Head pointed, mouth directed upward; Back brownish olive to steel-blue, partly depending on angle of light. 3 or 4 steel-blue lateral bands on sides separated by bright yellow or golden narrow bands. All fins reddish or blueish except pectorals, which are clear. *Male:* More slender; middle blue stripe straight. *Female:* Fuller, often somewhat larger. Middle blue stripe curved upward at caudal base.
LENGTH: 4-5 inches.
CARE: Lively and active; does well in community tank with other medium-large fishes of similar nature. Capable of swallowing small fishes. Well-planted, well-lit aquarium, preferably aerated. Best kept in schools. Large aquarium with plenty of swimming room is best. Water not critical unless extreme in pH or hardness. Temperature 70-80°F.—21-27°C.
FEEDING: Almost all fish foods. Live food, of course is preferred, especially for conditioning. Frozen shrimp and flake foods also very good.
BREEDING: 10-15 gallon aquarium; moderately soft neutral or slightly acid water (not critical).

Giant Danio

Temp. 78-80°F.—26-27°C. Spawns on bunched plants. Full female introduced into breeding tank followed by two males a day or two later will ordinarily spawn rather readily.

Flying Fox

ORDER: *Cypriniformes*   FAMILY: *Cyprinidae*

SCIENTIFIC NAME: *Epalzeorhynchus kallopterus* (Bleeker).

POPULAR NAME: **Flying Fox.**

RANGE: Borneo, Sumatra.

HABITAT: Clear and turbid streams with sand, gravel and silt bottoms; gravel bars.

DESCRIPTION: Elongated, slender body. Snout pointed with mouth beneath. Two small pairs of barbels. Back dark golden to fish-green. Intense black band from snout to caudal peduncle; bordered above by light, sometimes golden band. Fins of healthy, mature fish with reddish tinge; lips sometimes red.

LENGTH: 4 inches; rarely more with exceptional care.

CARE: Large, well-planted aquarium with bright lighting. Moderately soft water. Temp. 74-80°F.—23-27°C. Very lively, active fish; should be covered. Harmlessly aggressive towards own kind; peaceful towards others. Broad-leaved plants, roots, etc. used as resting site. Nibbles algae almost continuously when not resting or distracted by other food. A reasonably effective "algae-eater", also a fine control for planarians (flatworms).

FEEDING: A detritus feeder in nature. Live, frozen and dried foods, oatmeal. Occasional canned or boiled spinach or alfalfa rabbit food pellets desirable.

BREEDING: Unknown.

91

Red-tailed Shark

ORDER: *Cypriniformes*   FAMILY: *Cyprinidae*
SCIENTIFIC NAME: *Labeo bicolor* Smith.
POPULAR NAME: **Red-tailed Shark; Red-tailed Black Shark.**
RANGE: Thailand.
DESCRIPTION: Velvet black or charcoal on body, sometimes with black spot on mid-side just preceding dorsal; dorsal large, almost flag-like, usually erect; pectorals clear, ventrals and anal black. Caudal deeply forked; mercurochrome-red to velvet red. Two barbels. *Male:* Slender. *Female:* More robust.
LENGTH: 5-6 inches in aquarium; usually less.
CARE: Large community aquarium holding other active medium-sized fishes. Aquarium well-planted, moderately to well-lighted. Do not keep with shy or slow-moving species. Water moderately soft to medium-hard, pH neutral to slightly alkaline or somewhat acid. Temp. 72-80°F.—22-27°C.
FEEDING. Omnivorous. Fond of small live foods, frozen brine shrimp. Partly vegetarian; needs spinach, algae, alfalfa. Cooked oatmeal is appreciated. Small amounts of paprika in the diet intensify the red of the caudal fin.
BREEDING: Seldom bred. Mature at 3 inches.

Harlequin Shark

ORDER: *Cypriniformes* FAMILY: *Cyprinidae*
SCIENTIFIC NAME: *Labeo variegatus* (Pellegrin).
POPULAR NAME: **Harlequin Shark.**
RANGE: Upper Congo.
DESCRIPTION: Young fish are yellowish, marbled with brown, black and some reddish. Adults: Dark brown above, yellowish grey below. Sides dark brown-gold or brown with crimson spot on each scale. Sides and fins with gold, reddish and brown beautifully mingled in changing light. First dorsal rays elongated to a point.
LENGTH: 5-6 inches.
CARE: Good in collection of fishes able to care for themselves. Aggressive, often towards an individual fish. Large, brightly lit and well-planted aquarium, preferably with retreats available. Aeration desirable. Water conditions uncritical. Temperature 70-80°F.—21-27°C.
FEEDING: Omnivorous, large amounts of vegetable matter plus other foods. An algae eater, only much less efficient than most loricariids. Live, frozen and dried foods, boiled oatmeal, spinach and alfalfa pellets. Heavy feeder.
BREEDING: Unknown.
COMMENT: A striking, bold-natured show fish for the large aquarium in adult sizes.

ORDER: *Cypriniformes*   FAMILY: *Cyprinidae*

SCIENTIFIC NAME: *Rasbora borapetensis* H. M. Smith.

POPULAR NAME: **Red-tailed Rasbora; Black-lined Rasbora.**

RANGE: Thailand.

HABITAT: Bung Borapet marsh, Thailand, and adjacent rivers.

DESCRIPTION: A broad black lateral band from gill cover to caudal root, bordered above by bright golden-green band; a dark median dorsal stripe from head to caudal fin; a black stripe at base of anal fin. Caudal fin pink-based to red; other fins clear. *Male:* Caudal redder; lateral stripe slightly more distinct. *Female:* More robust.

LENGTH: 2 inches.

CARE: Good community fish with other small, active and peaceful fishes. Should be kept in groups or shoals. Well-planted aquarium desirable, but should have plenty of free swimming space. Water moderately soft and neutral to somewhat acid. Temperature 72-80°F.—22-27°C.

FEEDING: Prefers live foods, such as mosquito larvae, but accepts almost all foods.

BREEDING: Clean, bare aquarium with bunched natural or artificial spawning plants. Temp. about 80°F.—27°C. Aeration may stimulate spawning. Pair or trio (2 males, 1 female) of well-conditioned fish usually spawn without difficulty on plants, after which they should be removed to prevent egg-eating. Babies take infusoria, liquid fry food; next finest newly hatched brine shrimp.

Red-tailed Rasbora

ORDER: *Cypriniformes* FAMILY: *Cyprinidae*

SCIENTIFIC NAME: *Rasbora dorsiocellata* Duncker.

POPULAR NAME: **Eye-spot Rasbora.**

RANGE: Malay Peninsula; Sumatra.

HABITAT: Streams and pools.

DESCRIPTION: Body yellowish-silver, belly silvery-white. With reflected light, a fine olive-gold lateral band from gill cover to caudal root; often very obscure. Fins clear to yellowish; dorsal with conspicuous black spot edged w.th white or enamel-white. *Male:* Caudal pinkish or reddish at breeding. *Female:* More robust; belly more rounded.

LENGTH: 1½-2 inches.

CARE: Excellent, unobtrusive member of community aquarium of other small, peaceful fishes. Best kept in schools in well-planted, well-lit aquarium with ample swimming room. Lively and active; may nip long fins of slow-moving fishes; otherwise inoffensive. Subtle attractiveness complements other, brighter fishes. Water moderately soft, slightly to somewhat acid. Temperature in mid-70°'sF.–24°C., higher for breeding.

FEEDING: Almost all high quality foods. Especially fond of small living foods, frozen brine shrimp, etc. Mosquito larvae excellent for conditioning breeders.

BREEDING: Preferably rather soft, slightly acid to acid water. Temp. about 80°F.—27°C. Spawns

Eye-spot Rasbora

rather readily if well-conditioned, on bunched
natural or artificial plants in standard minnow
fashion. Babies raised accordingly.

Red Rasbora

ORDER: *Cypriniformes*   FAMILY: *Cyprinidae*
SCIENTIFIC NAME: *Rasbora heteromorpha* Duncker.
POPULAR NAME: **Red Rasbora; Harlequin Rasbora.**
RANGE: Malay Peninsula; Thailand; Sumatra.
HABITAT: Small streams, small still waterways.
DESCRIPTION: Body glowing salmon-red, dorsal and caudal deeper red. A large black triangle on

posterior half of body, outlined with golden. *Male:* More slender. *Female:* Lower corner of wedge less distinct.

VARIATIONS: Body hues may vary from deep red to dull orange, overcast with subtle violet. Water condition influences tone tremendously.

LENGTH: 2 inches; often less.

CARE: Community aquarium of similar-sized, peaceful fishes or containing only Red Rasbora. Aquarium should be roomy, thickly planted with *Cryptocoryne*, *Hygrophila* or other plant species of similar nature. Soft, somewhat acid water best, although tolerance is wide. If kept for prolonged periods in hard and/or alkaline water Red Rasbora reportedly become sterile. Schooling fish; should be kept in shoals. Temperature 72-80°F.—22-27°C.

FEEDING: All high quality small fish foods. Live and frozen foods should be regularly fed for conditioning breeders. Mosquito larvae excellent.

BREEDING: Spawns normally in groups on underside of plant leaves such as broad-leaved *Cryptocoryne* sp. Water must be very soft and acid, pH 5.6-6.4 or near. If aquarium is placed so that a few rays of morning sun shine inside, this is a definite stimulus to spawning. Breeding temp. around 80°F.—27°C. Parents usually will not molest eggs, but may eat young. Eggs hatch in 24-28 hours. Free-swimming babies need infusoria or liquid-type fry food. Success depends chiefly on water conditions.

ORDER: *Cypriniformes* FAMILY: *Cyprinidae*
SCIENTIFIC NAME: *Rasbora maculata* Duncker.
POPULAR NAME: **Spotted Rasbora; Pigmy Rasbora.**
RANGE: Southern Malay Peninsula; Singapore; Sumatra.
HABITAT: Ponds, ditches, small streams.
DESCRIPTION: Bright brick-red with greenish or olive sheen on back; sides yellowish-red; belly lighter. A large, conspicuous black spot behind pectorals at about eye-level, another smaller black blotch at anal base and on caudal root. Dorsal with black tip, dark front edge. Fins red to yellowish-red. *Male:* More slender, bright red, fins brighter. *Female:* More yellowish, more robust, belly more rounded.
LENGTH: 1 inch; males often less.
CARE: This tiny species best kept by itself or with other tiny, peaceful fishes such as Neon Tetras. A dark bottom is preferred, with moderately thick planting. Plenty of swimming room should be left. Best kept in schools. Water should be soft and acid. Aquarium need not be large; filtration desirable in order to keep water crystal clear. This species likes natural sunlight, which is a stimulant to spawning.
FEEDING: Small live foods preferred, such as newly hatched brine shrimp.
BREEDING: Condition pairs separately on copious live foods. Water must be soft and acid. Temp.

Spotted Rasbora

about 80°F.—27°C. Spawns on bunched plants. Remove parents after spawning. Hatching in 24-36 hours. Free-swimming babies can eat liquid fry food or finest brine shrimp.

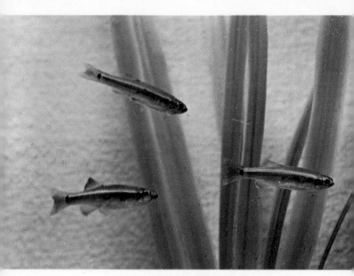

White Cloud Mountain Fish

ORDER: *Cypriniformes*   FAMILY: *Cyprinidae*

SCIENTIFIC NAME: *Tanichthys albonubes* Lin.

POPULAR NAME: **White Cloud Mountain Fish; White Cloud.**

RANGE: White Cloud Mountain, Canton, China.

HABITAT: Gorges near White Cloud Mountain.

DESCRIPTION: Body elongate, slightly compressed; reddish brown with bright golden greenish "neon" band from snout to caudal root. In young, band is more blue-green, resembling young Neon Tetras. Caudal red in middle; anal and dorsal with yellow at base, brilliant red outside. Belly whitish. A beautiful, active species. *Male:* More slender. *Female:* Plumper.

LENGTH: 1½ inches.

CARE: Excellent community aquarium occupant. Best kept in schools in presence of other small, active and harmless fishes. Temp. range extremely wide, 40-90°F.— 4-32°C. Water conditions widely acceptable. Bright or moderately bright, well-planted aquaria suitable. Can be kept outside year-round in some localities because of tolerance to low temperatures.

FEEDING: Almost any small food. Live; frozen; freeze-dried; high quality dried and flake foods.

BREEDING: Spawns readily on clumps of plants such as *Myriophyllum* or artificial spawning grass. Can also be bred in rod traps or over beds of marbles as for *Brachydanio* sp. Best breeding at 70-75°F.—21-25°C. Free-swimming babies eat infusoria or prepared substitute.

105

ORDER: *Cypriniformes*   FAMILY: *Cobitidae*
SCIENTIFIC NAME: *Acanthophthalmus kuhlii* (Cuvier & Valeniennes).
POPULAR NAME: **Giant Coolie Loach; Kuhli Loach**.
RANGE: Sumatra; Java. Sub-species more widespread.
HABITAT: Pools and streams, both clear and muddy.
DESCRIPTION: Numerous wide, dark bands with narrow salmon-pink to yellowish interspaces; belly salmon to yellow-pink. Heavier-bodied, larger than common "Coolie" (*A. semicinctus*). *Female:* Heavier than male.
LENGTH: Up to 4 inches.
CARE: Well-planted aquarium with hiding places under rocks, bark, in caves, etc. Excellent "scavenenger", but should be fed as any other fish. Aeration desirable. Moderately soft water; near neutral to moderately acid pH. Temp. 72-80°F.—22-27°C. *Acanthophthalmus* sp. indicate polluted, foul or overheated water by swimming nervously up and down aquarium glass. Retiring and shy under normal conditions, eventually becoming tame at feeding time. Tropical cobitids (loaches) should be handled carefully to avoid cuts and punctures from sharp, erectile, sub-orbital spines.
FEEDING: Omnivorous. Especially fond of pellet foods which sink rapidly, since these are strictly bottom feeders. Frozen foods, boiled oatmeal, etc.

Giant Coolie Loach; Kuhli Loach

BREEDING: Uncommon. Young Coolies of this genus appear sometimes in aquaria where numerous adults are kept. Eggs sometimes found under rocks, filters, etc.

Clown Loach

ORDER: *Cypriniformes*   FAMILY: *Cobitidae*
SCIENTIFIC NAME: *Botia macracantha* (Bleeker).
POPULAR NAME: **Clown Loach.**
RANGE: Borneo; Sumatra.
HABITAT: Moving streams as well as quieter waterways.
DESCRIPTION: A brilliantly beautiful fish seldom approached in its striking appearance by freshwater fishes. Brilliant red-orange to golden-orange body; three coal-black, wedge-shaped vertical bars, one through eye, one just preceding dorsal onto belly, and one through rear of dorsal onto anal. Ventrals, pectorals and caudal blood red.
LENGTH: Seldom more than 5 inches in aquarium; much more in nature.
CARE: Well-planted, larger community aquaria provided with caves, roots or rocks for seclusion. Can be kept in groups, although older and larger specimens tend to fight or at least establish rigid peck-orders. Water should be moderately soft to soft, and neutral to somewhat acid. Other water conditions will be tolerated, but these promote best health and appearance. Temp. 72-80°F.—22-27°C.
FEEDING: All live foods, especially worms. Large earthworms should be chopped. Fond of snails, especially red ramshorns. Some algae or other vegetation.
BREEDING: Impractical.

Ornate Catfish ; Ornate Chrysichthys

ORDER: *Siluriformes*   FAMILY: *Bagridae*
SCIENTIFIC NAME: *Chrysichthys ornatus* Boulenger.
POPULAR NAME: **Ornate Catfish; Ornate Chrysichthys.**
RANGE: Upper and middle Congo; Ubangi.
DESCRIPTION: Body elongate; 4 pairs of barbels; head flattened with very wide mouth. Body yellow to tan, with dark rust-brown to black blotches and spots; belly white or yellow-white. Adipose fin present. Caudal forked, with dark lengthwise bands on upper and lower lobes. Rather shy, especially until acclimatized.
LENGTH: 6 inches in aquarium.
CARE: Large, not too brightly lit aquarium, provided with rocks, roots or caves for hiding. Temp. 70-80°F.—21-27°C. A wide range of water conditions are apparently suitable, although extremes of pH and hardness should be avoided. Territorially competitive with other catfishes for choice cave locations, suggesting that an adequate number of such facilities be provided Otherwise peaceful with most fishes too large to be swallowed.
FEEDING: Live earthworms; beef heart; canned dog food (certain cheap dog foods contain too much starchy vegetable matter, causing cloudy water). Some specimens learn to accept boiled oatmeal, especially in presence of competition.
BREEDING: Unknown.

ORDER: *Siluriformes* FAMILY: *Siluridae*

SCIENTIFIC NAME: *Kryptopterus bicirrhis* (Cuvier & Valenciennes).

POPULAR NAME: **Glass Catfish; Ghost Glass Catfish; Indian Glass Catfish.**

RANGE: India; Greater Sunda Islands, Indonesia; Thailand.

HABITAT: Rivers; affluents.

DESCRIPTION: Dorsal very small, no adipose. Flesh crystal-clear, with bones and vertebral structure visible; vital organs enclosed in opaque sac. Two maxillary barbels. Anal extremely long-based, rippling almost ceaselessly; caudal forked, lower lobe usually slightly larger. A strikingly beautiful, delicate-looking but hardy and long-lived fish under good conditions. By reflected sunlight, sides sparkle a rainbow of spectral reflections.

LENGTH: 4 inches.

CARE: Should be kept in schools or groups in community or other sizeable, well-planted aquarium providing plenty of open swimming space. Peaceful and active with wide range of tolerance for water conditions. Keep with other gentle-natured, peaceful fishes. Temp. 72-82°F.—22-28°C. Aeration, filtration desirable.

FEEDING: Prefers small living foods, but will accept frozen and highest quality flake and dried foods. Also takes finely ground or blended beef heart.

Glass Catfish

Before grinding or otherwise preparing beef heart, remove all fat.
BREEDING: Unknown.

ORDER: *Siluriformes*　　　　　FAMILY: *Schilbeidae*
SCIENTIFIC NAME: *Schilbe mystus* (Linnaeus).
POPULAR NAME: **Mystus Catfish; African Glass Catfish.**
RANGE: Tropical Africa; Nile basin.
DESCRIPTION: 4 pairs of barbels, all rather short; no adipose; caudal deeply forked, lobes somewhat pointed. Silvery to smoke-grey or brownish with silvery sheen; dark blotch over pectorals, just behind gill cover. Sometimes with three dark bands running laterally the length of the body, the upper band extending onto upper caudal lobe. Bands become less distinct with increasing age and size.
LENGTH: 5-6 inches in aquarium; 1 foot in nature.
CARE: Preferably kept in groups of several; a free-swimming, open-water fish under suitable conditions. Moderate lighting, with adequate cover available, plus plenty of free-swimming space promote confidence. Overcrowded, overlit and sparsely furnished aquaria may make *Schilbe* lie motionless and inactive on aquarium floor, a completely unnatural reaction. Temp. 72-80°F.—22-27°C., pH and hardness content not critical. Excellent show fish with other lively, peaceful fishes. One caution; mouth quite large and capable of swallowing relatively sizeable fishes.
FEEDING: Omnivorous, with preference for meat-based or fish-based foods. Live worms; small fishes;

Mystus Catfish; African Glass Catfish

beef heart; canned or dried dog food; boiled oatmeal.
BREEDING: Unknown.

ORDER: *Siluriformes*　　　　FAMILY: *Mochokidae*

SCIENTIFIC NAME: *Synodontis angelicus* (Schilthuis).

POPULAR NAME: **Black Clown Upside-down Catfish; Polka-dot Upside-down Catfish.**

RANGE: Congo; tropical West Africa.

DESCRIPTION: Body velvet black; large white dots which in young may be yellowish, dispersed over body and belly. Fins with alternate black and white bars. Adipose rather large; black with white spots. Mouth beneath; mandibular barbels branched.

VARIATIONS: Black with white dots and small, sharply delineated, curved white bars over body, giving impression of black lace.

LENGTH: 6 inches or more; usually less.

CARE: Excellent, although rather retiring, show fish for large community aquarium. Generally peaceful, but occasionally fights with other *Synodontis*. Long-lived; the author has personally kept an individual over 15 years. Should have roomy aquarium provided with roots, caves or other hiding places. Aquarium may be planted, but swimming space should be ample. Crepuscular (twilight-active); often swims in inverted position. May hide in caves upside-down, belly against roof of cave.

FEEDING: Almost any food reaching bottom. Takes food in midwater, often upside-down, after acclima-

Black Clown Upside-down Catfish

tization. Live, frozen, pellet foods, beef heart, cooked oatmeal, etc.
BREEDING: Unknown. Sex distinctions not observed.

ORDER: *Siluriformes*   FAMILY: *Mochokidae*
SCIENTIFIC NAME: *Synodontis decorus* Boulenger.
POPULAR NAME: **Decorus Upside-down Catfish.**
RANGE: Upper Congo.
DESCRIPTION: Body silver white to tannish white; prominent black blotches on sides, back; humeral process rounded; three pairs of branched barbels. Dorsal with 3 or 4 black bars, first ray greatly elongated in older fish, rather filament-like reaching caudal or beyond. Caudal forked, lobes pointed, 3-4 black prominent bars on each lobe.
LENGTH: 8 inches; possibly more.
CARE: Well-planted aquarium or alternatively with plenty of roots, rockwork, caves, etc. Water not critical. Temp. 70-80°F.—21-27°C. Excellent community occupant; beautiful show fish. Retiring nature can be overcome by keeping with other *Synodontis*. Certain species, however, incompatible. Most fight harmlessly, although almost continuously unless enough cave-sites are present.
FEEDING: Almost all fish foods which sink. Heavy feeder, grows rapidly if well fed. Pellet type, tablet foods especially appreciated. Spinach or other vegetation occasionally beneficial. Large specimens fond of large earthworms.
BREEDING: Unknown.
COMMENTS: Large specimens sometimes make clearly audible "growling" noise.

118

Decorus Upside-down Catfish

ORDER: *Siluriformes* FAMILY: *Mochokidae*

SCIENTIFIC NAME: *Synodontis eupterus* Boulenger.

POPULAR NAME: **Feather-fin Catfish.**

RANGE: White Nile.

DESCRIPTION: Young rather ordinary, speckled, muddy appearance, and rather uninteresting; typical *Synodontis*. At maturity, body deepens and dorsal rays become prolonged, first rays reaching beyond adipose and in fine specimens, even past caudal. Caudal deeply forked, upper lobe prolonged into filament at maturity. Body rather mustard-grey, with numerous small, round spots of black. Fins handsomely barred light and dark; adipose spotted, large. Mandibular barbels feathered.

LENGTH: 6 or more inches.

CARE: Light-shy; retiring. Well-planted aquarium with numerous cave-sites, rocks, roots, etc., for retirement. Moderate lighting. Active during twilight (crepuscular) and darkness (nocturnal), swimming often in inverted position. Upper aquarium layers should have open swimming space. Water conditions uncritical; temp. 72-80°F. —22-27°C. Avoid keeping with notorious fin-nippers such as certain puffers (*Tetraodon*).

FEEDING: Heavy, omnivorous feeder with preference for animal matter such as live earthworms, other live food, frozen brine shrimp, beef heart, occasional vegetable matter, such as cooked spinach, algae, alfalfa rabbit food pellets. Fond of pellet-type food.

120

Feather-fin Catfish

BREEDING: Unknown.

COMMENT: An outstandingly beautiful show fish, becoming more spectacular with increasing age. Great longevity with large aquarium and good care; 10 years or more.

ORDER: *Siluriformes*   FAMILY: *Auchenipteridae*

SCIENTIFIC NAME: *Trachycorystes fisheri* Eigenmann.

POPULAR NAME: **Driftwood Catfish.**

RANGE: Northern South America; Panama.

DESCRIPTION: Belly rather creamy white; brown to dark brown on back and sides. Back and sides with numerous irregular black longitudinal flecks and streaks, most abundant dorsally. Caudal often with dark bar at base. *Male:* Head more concave in profile than female. *Female:* Head less concave.

LENGTH: 6 inches, usually less.

CARE: Shy and retiring; needs caves, roots or heavy vegetation in which to hide during day. Excellent nocturnal scavenger. If rooted stump is present, *T. fisheri* will often position itself motionless in head-up position in crotch of roots, almost perfectly camouflaged. Good in community aquarium with fishes down to half its own size.

FEEDING: Omnivorous. Gluttonous feeder, but food must be dropped within reach until acclimatized, since this fish is very reluctant at first to come into lighted area and compete for food. Beef heart, boiled oatmeal, pre-soaked dried dog food, etc. Smaller specimens somewhat less shy, eat any standard fish food, but such fare becomes impractical for very large specimens.

BREEDING: Unknown.

COMMENT: A most interesting fish for the collector of "oddball" catfishes.

Driftwood Catfish

"Pimelodella angelicus"

ORDER: *Siluriformes*   FAMILY: *Pimelodidae*

SCIENTIFIC NAME: *Pimelodus pictus* Steindachner.

POPULAR NAME: **"Pimelodella angelicus"** (a trade name).

RANGE: South America; Marañon, Peru.

DESCRIPTION: Body quite silver to silver-white. Maxillary barbels rather stiff-looking, reaching to adipose or to caudal, two other pairs of shorter barbels. Caudal forked; lobes pointed. Dark spots on bases of dorsal rays, tips of dorsal rays dark, giving dorsal a dark edging. Black or dark marking on back and sides; tip of adipose dark or black. Two dark spots at base of caudal, two or three black bars on lobes. Other fins whitish.

LENGTH: 3-4 inches.

CARE: Lively addition to well-planted community aquarium containing medium-sized to medium-large fishes. Most undemanding. Large aquarium with plenty of swimming room. Aeration, filtration desirable. Water non-critical. Temp. 70-80°F.— 21-27°C.

FEEDING: Omnivorous. Live food, especially medium or small earthworms. Fond of pellet and tablet food, also ground beef heart. Accepts almost any food reaching bottom.

BREEDING: Unknown.

COMMENT: One of most desirable of pimelodid catfishes. A striking example of beauty in simplest contrast.

125

ORDER: *Siluriformes*   FAMILY: *Callichthyidae*
SCIENTIFIC NAME: *Callichthys callichthys* (Linnaeus).
POPULAR NAME: **Callichthys; Armoured Catfish.**
RANGE: Northern South America.
HABITAT: Slow-moving or standing waters with soft bottom.
DESCRIPTION: Body elongate, rather lozenge-shaped. Head flattened dorsally. Dark grey-green to brown, with blueish or greenish sheen by reflected light. Fins grey or grey-brown, spotted; sometimes with orange border. *Male:* Brighter; pectoral spines heavier. *Female:* Slightly duller.
LENGTH: 5 inches or more.
CARE: Excellent show fish for large community aquarium in larger sizes. Can be kept with smaller fishes than most comparable-sized catfishes (within reason). Larger specimens will dig up all but well-anchored plants. Water uncritical. Temp. 70-80°F. —21-27°C. A soft bottom is appreciated, or one not containing sharp sand. Sharp-edged sand sometimes irritates barbels of callichthyids.
FEEDING: Almost anything edible, but especially fond of live food, such as medium-sized earthworms. Pellet foods appreciated. Ground beef heart good conditioner.
BREEDING: Bubble-nest builder. Male constructs nest beneath floating plants; water lilies, *Riccia*, etc. Male assumes brood care. Large aquarium recommended.

126

Callichthys; Armoured Catfish

Bronze Corydoras

ORDER: *Siluriformes*　　　　FAMILY: *Callichthyidae*
SCIENTIFIC NAME: *Corydoras aeneus* (Gill).
POPULAR NAME: **Bronze Corydoras.**
RANGE: Trinidad; Venezuela; Bolivia; Argentina.
HABITAT: Slow-moving streams, sometimes ponds.
DESCRIPTION: Dull, metallic olive to greenish gold on sides and back. Belly pinkish to grey white. Sides covered with bony armour plates. Adipose fin present. *Male:* More slender; darker green or olive. *Female:* More robust; belly rounded. Females often larger. In well-conditioned fish, comparative roundness of female's belly is apparent when viewed from beneath through glass-bottom tank.

LENGTH: 3 inches.

CARE: Excellent, efficient workers for the community aquarium. Small groups or schools of Bronze or other *Corydoras* search out uneaten scraps of food which might have escaped other inhabitants. Although often sold as "scavengers", they should not be relegated to such a role, since they enjoy prime fish food as much as any other fish. Water not excessively deep; moderately soft to slightly hard; pH around neutral. Not critical. Temperature 65-80°F.—18-27°C.

FEEDING: Live foods which reach bottom, frozen brine shrimp, etc. Especially fond of pellet or tablet-type food. Chopped earthworms excellent for conditioning breeders.

BREEDING: Large, adhesive eggs are pressed onto aquarium walls, plant leaves, etc., by female. One ripe female and two or three slender, active males may usually be induced to spawn in a bare 15-gallon aquarium filled two-thirds with moderately soft neutral water. Temperature fluctuations and lively aeration seem to be a stimulus to spawning. Some breeders prefer not to feed heavily-conditioned *Corydoras* in breeding aquarium, others continue to feed chopped worms, live or frozen brine shrimp and pellet or tablet food, removing any uneaten food with siphon. Remove breeders after spawning. Babies can be raised easily on fine powdered food, microworms and newly hatched brine shrimp.

ORDER: *Siluriformes*   FAMILY: *Callichthyidae*
SCIENTIFIC NAME: *Corydoras arcuatus* Elwin.
POPULAR NAME: **Skunk Corydoras; Arched Corydoras.**

RANGE: Amazon Basin.

HABITAT: Slow-moving waters; shallows of streams.

DESCRIPTION: Body cream to yellowish-grey; belly white. Broad, dark bar from mouth upward through eye and arching along dorsal surface to caudal, where it continues onto lower edge. Adipose present, sides with bony armour plates. *Male:* Usually smaller, more slender. *Female:* Larger, more robust. Belly of conditioned female obviously more rounded when viewed from beneath.

LENGTH: $2\frac{1}{2}$ inches.

CARE: Excellent, completely inoffensive community aquarium occupant with other small, peaceful fishes. Best kept in groups; helps keep aquarium free of uneaten food. The aquarist should see that some food gets to such bottom feeders as this and other *Corydoras* species. Moderately to well-planted aquarium, providing some open swimming space on bottom. Roots, rocks, caves appreciated. Temp. 73-77°F.—22-25°C. Water uncritical as to pH and hardness if not extreme.

FEEDING: Live or frozen food, pellet, tablet or other sinking foods. Chopped earthworms excellent conditioner.

Skunk Corydoras

BREEDING: Not easy. Heavy, well-conditioned female, two or three active, slender males. Spawning sometimes stimulated by dropping temperature to 65°F.—18°C., bringing back up next day.

Black-spotted Catfish

ORDER: *Siluriformes*   FAMILY: *Callichthyidae*
SCIENTIFIC NAME: *Corydoras melanistius* Regan.
POPULAR NAME: **Black-spotted Catfish; Saddle Catfish.**
RANGE: Northern South America; Rio Essequibo, Guyana.
HABITAT: Slow-moving waters.
DESCRIPTION: Body flesh-pink; body and fins sprinkled with dark spots. A black vertical band through eye, rather reminiscent of the "mask" of a

raccoon. Base and middle front portion of dorsal black, extending onto back and forming a "saddle". Adipose present; typical callichthyid bony plates on body. Armour plates less obvious in appearance than in many *Corydoras* species. *Male:* Somewhat more slender; reportedly with more pointed dorsal. *Female:* More robust, especially when viewed from beneath.

LENGTH: $2\frac{1}{2}$ inches.

CARE: Entertaining and useful member of community aquarium. Best kept in groups in well-planted aquarium with medium or small-sized, non-aggressive fishes. Water not critical, although potential breeders might best be maintained in moderately soft water. Helps clean up left-overs of food, but should be fed as any fish, not restricted to the life of a scavenger.

FEEDING: Live food, especially tubifex and chopped earthworms. Fond also of pellet and tablet-type food, as well as sunken flake and dried food of good quality.

BREEDING: Difficult. Seldom accomplished. Large eggs pasted to plants, glass by female. See *C. aeneus*.

Peppered Corydoras; Spotted Corydoras

ORDER: *Siluriformes*   FAMILY: *Callichthyidae*

SCIENTIFIC NAME: *Corydoras paleatus* (Jenyns).

POPULAR NAME: **Peppered Corydoras; Spotted Corydoras.**

RANGE: South-eastern Brazil; Argentina.

HABITAT: Slow-flowing waters.

DESCRIPTION: Sides with rows of bony armour plates or scutes; back olive-brown, marmorated and peppered with darker blotches; sides brownish grey to yellowish-green, peppered and mottled with darker. Belly yellowish-white to flesh-toned. Fins also spotted and speckled. (Photograph is a bit more blueish than usual.)

LENGTH: 3 inches. Males usually less.

CARE: Peaceful, excellent community fish with other small, peaceful fishes. Best kept in groups if possible. Active searcher for uneaten food left by others. Wide toleration for water conditions. Temp. 65-80°F.—18-27°C. As with other *Corydoras* species, capable of accessory atmospheric respiration in crowded or polluted situation.

FEEDING: Prefers live foods which reach bottom, but eats almost anything containing some animal matter. Pellet and tablet foods eaten enthusiastically. Chopped earthworms, frozen brine shrimp, white worms and bloodworms excellent for conditioning.

BREEDING: Easiest of callichthyid catfishes to breed. Two or three slender, energetic males placed in bare or established, unpopulated aquarium with well-rounded, robust female will usually spawn if well-conditioned. Aeration, temperature fluctuation, sometimes act as spawning inducement. Large, adhesive eggs are pasted to aquarium walls and plants (if present) by female. Well-fed fish often ignore eggs, but should be removed after spawning. Imminent spawning is apparent in activity and excitement of breeders. Spawns may be surprisingly large, considering the large egg size, as many as 200 or more with large females. Babies easily raised on liquid fry food, fine dried food and newly hatched fresh or frozen brine shrimp.

ORDER: *Siluriformes* FAMILY: *Loricariidae*
SCIENTIFIC NAME: *Loricaria filamentosa* Steindachner.
POPULAR NAME: **Whiptail; Whiptail Loricaria.**
RANGE: Canelos, Ecuador; Rio Magdalena, Colombia.
HABITAT: Creeks, streams; usually clear, swift and shallow water with gravel, sand or pebble bottom.
DESCRIPTION: Body long, very slender. Upper caudal ray produced into long filament (*filamentosa*). Upper side greyish to yellowish brown, with numerous dark blotches, often appearing as irregular rings on posterior half of body. Caudal filament often alternately light and dark. Sides armoured with bony plates; also belly. Belly yellowish to white. Fins with irregular dark markings. *Male:* Tubercles on head.
LENGTH: 10 inches; usually much less.
CARE: Clear, well-planted and brightly lit aquarium, preferably large. Peaceful even with smaller fishes. Although the fish is crepuscular and somewhat light-shy, bright lighting promotes growth of algae upon which *L. filamentosa* will graze almost continuously after acclimatization to aquarium living. Water about neutral, not too hard. Temperature 72-80°F.—22-27°C.
FEEDING: Almost any food reaching bottom. Vegetation required such as algae, spinach (cooked), alfalfa pellets.

Whiptail; Whiptail Loricaria

BREEDING: Uncommon but possible. Spawn is placed on rocks or in crevices; male assumes brood care. Spawning site pre-cleaned by both parents.

Spotted Sucker Catfish

ORDER: *Siluriformes*   FAMILY: *Loricariidae*

SCIENTIFIC NAME: *Pterygoplichthys gibbiceps* (Kner).

POPULAR NAME: **Spotted Sucker Catfish.**

RANGE: Amazon.

HABITAT: Rivers and streams; lakes.

DESCRIPTION: *Pterygoplichthys* is comprised of *Hypostomus*-like loricariids which possess over ten dorsal rays and granular snouts. *P. gibbiceps* is apparently the most common Amazonian species. Light or dark brown; covered everywhere with large, dark spots interspersed with similar smaller spots. Spots on belly large and regular. Pectorals extending beyond base of ventrals; all fins covered with large dark spots. Dorsal quite large, almost sail-like, with 12-14 rays. Snout naked in young, granular in adults; ventral surface also granular in adults but not in young. Outer caudal rays thick and elongated. Upper caudal ray sometimes yellowish. Slightly hump-backed in appearance from profile.

LENGTH: 8-10 inches in aquarium; twice this in nature.

CARE: Large, brightly lighted aquarium with other large fishes. Rocky caves, roots and sturdy, well-anchored plants appreciated. Good algae eater. Temperature 70-82°F.—21-28°C. Water conditions non-critical.

FEEDING: Omnivorous. Does well on boiled oatmeal with occasional spinach, alfalfa pellets. Game fish (hatchery) food eagerly eaten by almost all lori-cariids.

BREEDING: Unknown.

Lyretail

ORDER: *Atheriniformes*   FAMILY: *Cyprinodontidae*
SCIENTIFIC NAME: *Aphyosemion australe* (Rachow).
POPULAR NAME: **Lyretail; Lyretail Killie; Cape Lopez (or Cap Lopez) Lyretail.**
RANGE: West Africa; Cape Lopez area, Equatorial Africa.
HABITAT: Small bodies of water.
DESCRIPTION: *Male:* Body brownish red sprinkled with red spots; gill cover and shoulder region greenish to blueish. Dorsal and anal flag-like,

with white tips; inner portion reddish-rust to violet. Caudal lyre-shaped with lobes elongated; middle delicate green to blueish, with red spots. Upper, lower borders reddish, tips white. (Typical fish much more brown-to-golden in appearance; not as blue as in photograph.) *Female:* Plain, fins rounded. Brownish.

LENGTH: 2-2½ inches.

CARE: Easily kept in small container in pairs or trios (1 male, 2 females) containing rather soft, mildly acid water. A teaspoon of sea salt to every gallon or two of water is beneficial. Bunched plants such as *Utricularia minor* or *Riccia*, or artificial plants of similar nature seem to lessen tendency to leap out. Fish should be covered, however. Temperature rather cool, 65-75°F.—18-24°C. Lighting not too bright; dark bottom.

FEEDING: Live foods preferred. Mosquito larvae, bloodworms, etc. Brine shrimp, freeze-dried and some flake foods accepted.

BREEDING: Well-fed trios or pairs will produce a few eggs daily attached to floating plants. Eggs large and readily visible; rather tough and can be removed carefully with fingers or forceps to be placed in another container for hatching. Alternatively, pieces or bunches of plants may be removed with eggs attached or parent fish can be removed after 10 days or so of spawning. Eggs hatch 12-14 days ordinarily. Babies can take newly hatched brine shrimp and grow quite rapidly.

Blue Gularis

ORDER: *Atheriniformes*   FAMILY: *Cyprinodontidae*
SCIENTIFIC NAME: *Aphyosemion sjoestedti* (Lönnberg)
(formerly known as *A. coeruleum*).
POPULAR NAME: **Blue Gularis.**
RANGE: Cameroon; Nigeria.
DESCRIPTION: *Male:* Upper side reddish brown overcast with olive. Carmine to brownish red spots and streaks on head and sides, over bright blue-green to blue background. Latter half of sides vertically barred with red or red-brown over blue-ish to blue-green or bright olive. Dorsal blue-green to yellow-green with red spots. Anal blue, yellow-based. Caudal produced into three points: upper portion blue-green with red streaks; middle yellow; lower blue to pale blue. *Female:* Plainer; fins rounded.
LENGTH: 4-4¾ inches. One of the largest cyprinodonts.
CARE: Best kept in pairs in not too brightly lit aquarium providing retreats for the female. Aquarium must be covered; exceptional jumper. Water moderately soft, neutral to rather acid, especially for breeding. Males aggressive. A teaspoon or two of sea salt per gallon beneficial. Temperature 68-75°F.—20-24°C.
FEEDING: Prefers live food. Small or medium earthworms, mealworms excellent cultured food sources. Also accepts frozen, freeze-dried foods well.
BREEDING: Spawns in peat bottom-soil. Incubation about 4-8 weeks, more or less. Annual species.
COMMENT: This species extremely variable.

143

ORDER: *Atheriniformes*   FAMILY: *Cyprinodontidae*
SCIENTIFIC NAME: *Aphyosemion striatum* (Boulenger)
("*A. lujae* Boulenger"?).
POPULAR NAME: **Striated Aphyosemion.**
RANGE: N. Gabon; Congo.
DESCRIPTION: *Male:* Body olive above to blueish on sides. Several rows of carmine spots on sides, separated by olive or merging into longitudinal bands. Dorsal and anal edged with carmine and with carmine median streak. Caudal rounded or with upper rays forming short filament, spotted with carmine; carmine and white streak above and below (according to Boulenger). *Female:* Plainer.
LENGTH: 2 inches.
CARE: Moderately lighted, well-covered aquarium. Best kept with own kind in pairs. Water reasonably soft and neutral to somewhat acid. Some killie experts recommend hard, alkaline water for maintaining fish, moving them to soft and acid water with similar mineral content for breeding. Temperature 68-75°F.—20-24°C.
FEEDING: Prefers live foods, especially insects. Will accept high quality dried foods, freeze-dried and frozen foods. These should be supplemented, however, with occasional living food.
BREEDING: Spawns in layer of peat on aquarium floor.

144

Striated Aphyosemion

Argentine Pearl Fish

ORDER: *Atheriniformes*   FAMILY: *Cyprinodontidae*
SCIENTIFIC NAME: *Cynolebias belotti* Steindachner.
POPULAR NAME: **Argentine Pearl Fish.**
RANGE: La Plata Basin, South America.
HABITAT: Small pools and streams subject to periodic dessication.
DESCRIPTION: *Male:* Back dark blue; sides dark blue or grey-blue. Small pearl-like spots over head, body and bases of vertical fins. Vertical fins blue-grey, anal dark-edged. Pectoral pale blueish. Dark vertical stripe through eye. *Female:* Yellowish brown, dark brown spots. Usually smaller.
LENGTH: $2\frac{1}{2}$-$3\frac{3}{4}$ inches.
CARE: Best kept with own kind. If more than one male to aquarium, cover should be provided by heavy planting. Water moderately soft, somewhat acid. Dark bottom preferable, inch or two of peat ideal. Life span short, usually less than one year. Roomy aquarium. Temp. 72-76°F.—22-25°C. Higher temperatures may shorten life span considerably.
FEEDING: Live food, frozen, freeze-dried. May be alternated with best dried and flake foods. Heavy feeders.
BREEDING: Bottom spawners. Pair "dives" deeply into peat; deposits eggs. Spawning activity very lively and pair can be moved to spawn in several aquaria. After removing breeders, water is lowered and peat semi-dried; stored in plastic bags or other containers. Incubation period about 8 weeks. Eggs hatch upon addition of soft water. Babies take infusoria.

147

ORDER: *Atheriniformes*   FAMILY: *Cyprinodontidae*
SCIENTIFIC NAME: *Cynolebias whitei* Myers.
POPULAR NAME: **White's Pearl Fish; White's Cynolebias.**
RANGE: Brazil, around Rio de Janeiro.
HABITAT: Small bodies of water subject to periodic dessication.
DESCRIPTION: *Male:* Back brownish, sides brownish to blueish; numerous bright "pearl-spots" on body. Dorsal and anal elongated red to red-brown with light spots. *Female:* Rather plain; brownish with black spot at mid-side and at caudal root. Smaller.
LENGTH: 2½-3 inches.
CARE: Best kept with own kind in roomy aquarium. Water moderately soft to soft, rather acid to neutral. Peat bottom, rather deep layer for spawning. Heavy planting desirable if more than one male present. Annual fish; life span less than 1 year.
FEEDING: Heavy feeder; prefers live food. Insects or insect larvae ideal. Frozen brine shrimp, blood-worms etc. Highest quality flake, dried foods may supplement. There are indications that alternating dried and live foods is quite beneficial procedure.
BREEDING: Pair spawns deeply in peat or other bottom soil. Spawning quite lively; well-fed fish produce numerous eggs in season. Peat or egg-laden soil semi-dried, stored as for *Nothobranchius* or *C. belotti*. Incubation about 8 weeks. Addition of fresh water causes hatching, usually within hours. Babies take finest foods almost immediately. Growth rapid.

White's Pearl Fish

ORDER: *Atheriniformes*   FAMILY: *Cyprinodontidae*

SCIENTIFIC NAME: *Epiplatys annulatus* (Boulenger).

POPULAR NAME: **Banded Toothcarp; Banded Killie.**

RANGE: Sierra Leone; Boffia of Lower Guinea to Monrovia, Liberia.

HABITAT: Swamp-like areas of forests or open land, in hot, often stagnant and shallow water.

DESCRIPTION: Lemon yellow, with four broad black rings; dorsal and anal black and yellow or red. Caudal with central rays produced; two red or orange streaks from upper and lower caudal base connected with third red streak from middle of caudal base; junction at posterior portion of extended rays. Remainder of caudal blueish. *Female:* Plainer.

LENGTH: 1½ inches.

CARE: Best kept with own kind in small, well-covered aquarium. Water moderately soft and acid, especially for breeding. Temp. 68-78°F.—20-26°C.

FEEDING: Prefers small live foods such as mosquito larvae, *Drosophila*, brine shrimp. Freeze-dried, frozen foods acceptable.

BREEDING: Spawns on bunches of floating plants. Not easy. Babies are smallest of newborn killies, requiring microscopic food, such as rotifers, for a couple of weeks before taking newly hatched shrimp.

Banded Toothcarp; Banded Killie

Chevalier's Epiplatys

ORDER: *Atheriniformes*   FAMILY: *Cyprinodontidae*
SCIENTIFIC NAME: *Epiplatys chevalieri* (Pellegrin).
POPULAR NAME: **Chevalier's Epiplatys.**
RANGE: Congo.
HABITAT: Sluggish or standing surface waters.
DESCRIPTION: *Male:* Olive green to brown-red
above; sides brass-yellow to greenish, lighter

below. Sides with longitudinal rows of bright red spots, so close on lower part of body that spots run together. Dorsal, upper caudal spotted with red; middle caudal rays prolonged; lower rays produced to point. *Female:* Rather plain. Rows of brown-red spots.

LENGTH: 2-2½ inches.

CARE: Large-surfaced aquarium with floating vegetation, with other similar-sized fishes which occupy middle and lower layers. *Epiplatys* occupies upper, working a harmonious community situation. May also be kept with own species. Water non-critical for maintenance, but should be slightly acid, not too hard for breeding. Aquarium should be covered at all times. Temp. 72-78°F.—22-26°C. Avoid heavy aeration which overly disturbs the surface.

FEEDING: Live food preferred. Frozen, freeze-dried and best flake foods accepted. Mosquito larvae excellent.

BREEDING: Spawns on nylon mops or floating bunches of plants. Trios (1 male, 2 females) or pairs will produce several eggs daily for 2-3 weeks if well fed. Eggs can be removed daily; young rather delicate. Infusoria or liquid fry food may be followed by brine shrimp.

Red-finned Nothobranchius

ORDER: *Atheriniformes*   FAMILY: *Cyprinodontidae*
SCIENTIFIC NAME: *Nothobranchius melanospilus* (Pfeffer).
POPULAR NAME: **Red-finned Nothobranchius.**
RANGE: Longo Bay, Tanzania; Seychelles Islands.
HABITAT: Small coastal streams.
DESCRIPTION: *Male:* Caudal dark red, black-edged.
Dorsal, anal dark-edged with light outer edge; red
or red-based. Sides blue to blue-green; scales
red-edged; pectorals reddish-clear with blue border.

Striking. *Female:* Brownish; posterior part of body with black or dark spots.

LENGTH: 2 inches.

CARE: Best kept with own kind. More than one male to an aquarium calls for heavy planting and/or other abundant cover, since male *Nothobranchius* spp. are quite aggressive. A true annual, life span one year or less. Aquarium should have peat bottom, soft, slightly acid water, especially for breeding. Some authorities recommend holding non-breeding killies of this and other species in hard, alkaline water for disease resistance. A teaspoon or two of sea salt per gallon of aquarium water is beneficial, especially in very soft water. Temp. 68-75°F.—20-24°C. Higher temperature may shorten life span.

FEEDING: Live food best, especially insects or insect larvae. Frozen, freeze-dried (especially loose-pack) and some dried food accepted; probably beneficial.

BREEDING: Not difficult with proper handling, but requires patience. Well-fed fish spawn in bottom (peat) soil. Peat, with eggs, removed, semi-dried and stored in plastic bags for about three months. During this time they should remain in a dark location at 68-77°F.—20-25°C. For hatching, place still-damp soil in aquarium and add cool (not cold) water, enough to float the peat. Peat should be stirred gently in to assure saturation; babies should hatch in 3-4 days. After this, soil may be re-dried, stored another month and "hatched" again. This may even be done a third time. This is the recommended method of one of the world's foremost killie breeders, Col. Scheel. Babies can immediately take newly hatched brine shrimp; they grow at an almost unbelievable rate.

ORDER: *Atheriniformes*   FAMILY: *Cyprinodontidae*
SCIENTIFIC NAME: *Nothobranchius rachovii* Ahl.
POPULAR NAME: **Rachow's Nothobranchius.**
RANGE: Mozambique.
HABITAT: Pools which become periodically dessicated.
DESCRIPTION: *Male:* Red-orange anteriorly, with turquoise to metallic powder-blue spots and streaks becoming progressively more prominent rearwards. Anal and dorsal turquoise-to-blue with prominent red to red-brown spots and streaks. Caudal black-edged, red band inside black. Forward half of caudal with pattern similar to dorsal and anal. Strikingly beautiful. *Female:* Smaller; much less brilliant.
LENGTH: 2-2½ inches.
CARE: Best kept with own kind. Males aggressive and if more than one male is to be kept to an aquarium plenty of cover must be available. Aquarium well covered. Large quarters not required; 2-4 gallons plenty for pair or trio. Water soft, somewhat acid, especially for breeding. Temp. 68-78°F.—20-26°C.
FEEDING: Live food preferred, such as mosquito

Rachow's Nothobranchius

larvae, bloodworms, fruit flies (*Drosophila*). Frozen, freeze-dried, highest quality prepared foods acceptable, although live food should be provided as often as possible.

BREEDING: Soft, somewhat acid water. Layer of peat on bottom. *Nothobranchius* spp. spawn in bottom soil which must then be semi-dried and stored for about seven months. After incubation period, add enough cool (64°F.—18°C.) water so peat floats. Eggs hatch from a few hours to 3 or 4 days after addition of water. Babies can take brine shrimp immediately.

ORDER: *Atheriniformes*   FAMILY: *Cyprinodontidae*
SCIENTIFIC NAME: *Pachypanchax playfairi* (Günther).
POPULAR NAME: **Playfair's panchax.**
RANGE: Seychelles Islands; Zanzibar.
HABITAT: Fresh and brackish water.
DESCRIPTION: Brownish with green overcast; belly lighter. Several longitudinal bands, rather indistinct; with red spots also in rows on sides; dorsal, anal and caudal yellowish, with small red or dark spots. Anal and caudal with dark edge. *Male:* More prominently marked. *Female:* Plainer; dark spot on dorsal.
LENGTH: 3-4 inches.
CARE: Hardy, but nasty in temperament. Best kept in well-planted, covered aquarium with own kind, although may be kept with other aggressive fishes of same size and requirements if plenty of retreats available, especially floating plants in which to take refuge. Young less aggressive than older. Water conditions widely variable; addition of 1 teaspoon or so of sea salt or rock salt per gallon recommended. Temperature 68-78°F.—20-26°C.
FEEDING: Prefers live or frozen food, but will accept almost any animal-based food.
BREEDING: Spawns in floating bunched or other plants, nylon mops, etc. Will eat eggs unless well-fed. Eggs hatch 10-12 days; babies eat newly hatched shrimp.
COMMENT: Scales of male *P. playfairi* sometimes stand out strangely, almost as if symptomatic of the disease known as "dropsy".

Playfair's panchax

Green Rivulus; Cuban Rivulus

ORDER: *Atheriniformes*   FAMILY: *Cyprinodontidae*
SCIENTIFIC NAME: *Rivulus cylindraceus* Poey.
POPULAR NAME: **Green Rivulus; Cuban Rivulus.**
RANGE: Cuba.
HABITAT: Middle and upper layers of flowing streams.
DESCRIPTION: *Male:* Olive brown, back brownish. Belly yellow to orange, also throat. Indistinct dark band from snout through eye to caudal root. A deep blue blotch just behind gill cover. Sides with red or red-brown spots and blotches; sometimes with green spots. Fins yellow; anal, dorsal and caudal spotted. Anal dark-edged. *Female:* Much plainer; distinct ocellated spot on upper caudal root.
LENGTH: 2-2½ inches.
CARE: A rather active killie which must be covered, since it jumps amazingly well. May be kept in community with similar-sized fishes. Well-lit, well-planted aquarium preferred; some floating plants. Water completely non-critical. Temperature 70-78°F.—21-26°C. May "climb" out of water onto floating plants for short periods.
FEEDING: Live or frozen foods best. Freeze-dried foods acceptable, as well as highest quality flakes.
BREEDING: Not difficult. Spawns in nylon mops or floating plants. Eggs hatch in 12-14 days. Babies eat newly hatched brine shrimp.

ORDER: *Atheriniformes*   FAMILY: *Cyprinodontidae*
SCIENTIFIC NAME: *Roloffia occidentalis* (Lönnberg).
Previously known as *Aphyosemion sjoestedti*.
POPULAR NAME: **Golden Pheasant.**
RANGE: Sierra Leone, Africa.
HABITAT: Fresh, sometimes brackish pools, puddles.
DESCRIPTION: Strikingly beautiful; rather large for
killie (cyprinodont). *Male:* Back golden-red; sides
with bright golden-yellow lateral band, with red
above and below. Throat and lower gill covers
indigo with irregular bright red and gold on upper
opercular. Dorsal red at base with pale edge; anal
red and blue with pale edge. Pectorals and ventrals
blueish or reddish with pale edge in older fish.
Female: Golden.
LENGTH: To 3 inches.
CARE: Well-planted aquarium providing cover for
pair or more of this species. Large quarters not
required. Water soft and somewhat acid; temp. not
too warm, 65-75°F.—18-24°C. Dark bottom preferred, such as peat moss. Predatory. Salt beneficial,
1 teaspoon per gallon.
FEEDING: Preferably live food such as mosquito
larvae, tubifex, bloodworms or very small to
medium earthworms. Frozen, freeze-dried foods.
Occasional flake foods of highest quality, otherwise
live or foregoing substitutes.
BREEDING: Requires patience. Spawning not difficult, but eggs take 7 months or more to mature
properly. Eggs are laid in bottom soil (peat moss)

162

Golden Pheasant

which is removed, dried until just damp, and stored
in plastic bags or jars to retain some moisture.
After 7 or more months, add rain or distilled water to
the resulting culture. Fry often appear within hours
and should be hatched at least by next day. If not,
add small pinch of skim milk or dried fish food,
which create bacteria and apparently aid in
releasing unborn fry from eggs. Newly hatched
brine shrimp can be taken immediately. Growth
from this point is astonishing!

ORDER: *Atheriniformes*   FAMILY: *Poeciliidae*

SCIENTIFIC NAME: *Poecilia* species (aquarium-developed strain possibly involving hybridization of several species; almost certainly *P. latipinna* and *P. sphenops*).

POPULAR NAME: **Lyretail Black Mollie.**

RANGE: Southern U.S.; Mexico.

DESCRIPTION: Velvet black. Lyre-shaped tail. Pectoral, ventral and anal fins often disproportionately large. *Male:* Gonopodium (breeding organ) present. *Female:* Plumper, often larger.

VARIATIONS: Numerous. Fin size quite variable, especially dorsal. Purity of black, as opposed to "marbling" quite variable.

LENGTH: 3 inches or more.

CARE: Moderately hard, slightly alkaline water is best, preferably with a teaspoon of salt added per gallon. Well-planted, well-lighted aquarium, preferably receiving some sunlight. Temperature should be rather warm: 75-80°F.—24-27°C.

FEEDING: Almost all fish foods. Some vegetation essential. Sunlight promotes algal growth, which all Mollies pick at continuously. Substitutes such as cooked spinach, alfalfa rabbit food pellets, etc. Alfalfa pellets can be pulverized in blender (dry) and mixed with other dry food or used separately. Small, frequent feedings are best.

BREEDING: Livebearer, periodically producing live young. Various strains should be kept separately to preserve purity.

Lyretail Black Mollie

Marbled Lyretail Mollie

ORDER: *Atheriniformes*　　　　FAMILY: *Poeciliidae*

SCIENTIFIC NAME: *Poecilia* species (aquarium developed strain probably involving hybridization of *P. latipinna* and other(s)).

POPULAR NAME: **Marbled Lyretail Mollie; Marbled Sailfin Lyretail Mollie.**

RANGE: Southern U.S.; Mexico.

DESCRIPTION: Grey-green, speckled rather indiscriminately or "marbled" with black. Lyre-shaped tail or caudal fin. Other fins large. *Male:* Gonopodium present. *Female:* Plumper; more robust; often larger. Marble Mollies are intermediate between the green and black forms, marbling being caused by an abundance of melanophores or black pigment cells. Through selective breeding, pure blacks were developed. Marble Mollies at times produce black or near-black offspring; on the other hand, marble babies may be produced by blacks. Some of these may later turn black.

LENGTH: 3 inches or more.

CARE: Moderately hard and alkaline water. Well-planted, brightly lit aquarium, preferably receiving some sunlight. Temp. 75-80°F.—24-27°C. Aeration and filtration beneficial, almost essential for reasonable growth in aquarium. A teaspoon of rock salt or sea salt to each gallon or two is desirable. Water for mollies and most poeciliids should have frequent partial changes, should not be allowed to turn "yellow".

FEEDING: All foods. Some vegetation essential.

BREEDING: Livebearer. See other *Poecilia* sp.

167

Guppy ; Millions Fish

ORDER: *Atheriniformes*   FAMILY: *Poeciliidae*
SCIENTIFIC NAME: *Poecilia reticulata* (Peters).
POPULAR NAME: **Guppy ; Millions Fish.**
RANGE: Venezuela; Trinidad; Barbados; Guyana;
northern Brazil; introduced into numerous tropics
of the world.
HABITAT: Fresh, brackish ditches, creeks, swamps,
etc.
DESCRIPTION: *Male:* Tremendously variable in
form. Numerous standardized combinations of
finnage and patterns; its hues seem to embrace
the entire spectrum. Photograph illustrates one
of these forms. Caudal so enormously produced in
some specimens as to make. swimming difficult.
Female: Larger bodied, much plainer in form.
Greyish to yellowish brown. Fins plain, although
fancy strains have caudal pattern in some cases.
LENGTH: *Male:* 1¼-1½ inches. *Female:* 2 inches.
CARE: Excellent in community with other small
fishes. Ceaselessly active. Unexcelled beginner's
fish, probably having started more hobbyists than
any other species. For developing or maintaining
good stock, numerous separate containers may be
necessary for isolation. Temp. 65-85°F.—18-29°C.
Sensitive to rapid chilling.
FEEDING: All fish foods. Live food or frozen food as
well as vegetation beneficial.
BREEDING: Livebearer. Babies escape into heavy
floating vegetation or can be saved in "breeding
trap". Parents eat young if given opportunity.

169

Giant Sailfin Mollie

ORDER: *Atheriniformes* FAMILY: *Poeciliidae*

SCIENTIFIC NAME: *Poecilia velifera* (Regan).

POPULAR NAME: **Giant Sailfin Mollie** (after *Mollienesia* which was the former generic name); **Green Sailfin**.

RANGE: Yucatan, Mexico.

HABITAT: Brackish and fresh waters of coastal area and river mouths.

DESCRIPTION: *P. velifera* and its near relative, the more common *P. latipinna*, are quite similar in appearance, the distinguishing character being the dorsal fin ray count; about 15 in *P. latipinna*, about 18 in *P. velifera*, which is also larger. *Male:* With magnificent sail-like fins; typical poeciliid breeding organ consisting of a modification of the anal fin; tank-raised males with much smaller dorsal. Body olive to yellow-green with blueish; lace-like pattern of dark spots alternating with iridescent blue to light green spots; dorsal and caudal with lace-like patterns; edged often in bright orange. *Female:* Plainer although similar; dorsal smaller; heavy-bodied.

LENGTH: To 5 inches in nature.

CARE: Large, well-planted, well-lighted aquaria. Water preferably at least moderately hard and alkaline. A teaspoon of rock salt or two to the gallon beneficial. Temp. 74-80°F.—23-27°C. Do not overcrowd.

FEEDING: Algae, vegetation. Most food. Feed often.

BREEDING: Livebearer. Place female in advance in heavily planted aquarium. No breeding traps.

171

ORDER: *Atheriniformes*   FAMILY: *Poeciliidae*
SCIENTIFIC NAME: *Poecilia velifera* (Regan).
POPULAR NAME: **Lyretail Green Sailfin Mollie.**
RANGE: Yucatan, Mexico. (The lyretail form is a domestic development not found in nature.)
DESCRIPTION: Body grey-green; lyre-shaped tail or caudal fin. Other fins except dorsal more produced than in wild form. *Male:* Typical poeciliid modification of anal fin into intromittent organ. In some instances, line breeding for mutated enlargement or modification of fins has caused impairment of the functional ability of the male organ. Dorsal larger than female. *Female:* More robust; dark "gravid" spot visible at vent when pregnant.
LENGTH: 4 inches; smaller than wild *P. velifera.*
CARE: Large, heavily-planted and well-lit aquarium, receiving some natural sunlight if possible. Moderately hard, somewhat alkaline to neutral water. Addition of 1 teaspoon of rock or sea salt per gallon beneficial. Aeration and filtration desirable. Do not overcrowd.
FEEDING: Frequent, small feedings of most fish foods in combination with vegetable matter. Vegetable foods may consist of canned or cooked spinach, commercially available "Mollie Food", algae or rabbit food pellets, either crushed or blended. All forms of mollies are at least partial vegetarians.
BREEDING: Livebearers. Mollie babies quite large at birth, immediately able to eat fine solid food.

Lyretail Green Sailfin Mollie

Green Swordtail ; Mexican Swordtail

ORDER: *Atheriniformes*   FAMILY: *Poeciliidae*
SCIENTIFIC NAME: *Xiphophorus helleri* Heckel.
POPULAR NAME: **Green Swordtail ; Mexican Swordtail.**
RANGE: Southern Mexico; Guatemala.
HABITAT: Lowland streams emptying into Gulf of Mexico.
DESCRIPTION: *Male:* Lower caudal rays greatly elongated, forming a "sword"; back and sides greenish or blueish-grey; a shining greenish area from snout to caudal, accompanied by a reddish band. Quite variable in tone due to generations of aquarium breeding, the Green Swordtail is still a magnificent fish. Sword black-edged above and below, almost as long as the body in fine males. *Female:* Similar; much heavier and without sword. Sex-changes occur occasionally; females which have borne young develop male characteristics (sword; gonopodium). Often exceedingly large, these specimens are usually apparently sterile.
LENGTH: 5 inches in nature; much less in aquarium.
CARE: Excellent community fish in well-planted aquarium with other similar-sized fishes. Water moderately hard and alkaline, although considerable variation of water quality will be tolerated. Keep covered. Temperature 70-80°F.—21-27°C.
FEEDING: All fish foods. Some vegetable matter.
BREEDING: Livebearer. Large females may have 100 or more young at one time. Provide heavy floating plant cover for newborn; parents will eat them without this protection or other.

175

Red Swordtail

ORDER: *Atheriniformes* FAMILY: *Poeciliidae*

SCIENTIFIC NAME: *Xiphophorus* species, predominantly *X. helleri* Heckel which was hybridized with *X. maculatus* (Gunther) to increase the number of varieties available in the former.

POPULAR NAME: **Red Swordtail.**

RANGE: Southern Mexico; Guatemala.

HABITAT: Lowland streams emptying into Gulf of Mexico.

DESCRIPTION: *Male:* Lower caudal rays greatly elongated into a sword-like appendage. Body brick red to velvet or blood red; sword yellow-green to orange, edged with fine black line. Sword in some varieties same as body coloration; no black edge. Male poeciliid breeding organ or gonopodium present. *Female:* Much heavier, more robust; no sword or gonopodium. Dark spot visible at vent of pregnant female.

LENGTH: 4 inches or less.

CARE: Roomy, well-planted community or sword-tail aquarium with moderately hard, alkaline water. Temp. 70-80°F.—21-27°C. Excellent jumper; keep all swordtails covered. For purity of coloration do not mix swordtail varieties.

FEEDING: All fish foods, although some vegetable matter such as commercial "Mollie Food" should be given.

BREEDING: Livebearer. Female should be placed in separate aquarium provided with numerous floating plants. Should not be moved too near delivery time. Babies can eat newly hatched brine shrimp.

177

Gold Platy

ORDER: *Atheriniformes*   FAMILY: *Poeciliidae*
SCIENTIFIC NAME: *Xiphophorus maculatus* (Günther).
POPULAR NAME: **Gold Platy; Gold Moon; Gold Moon-fish.**
RANGE: Southern Mexico, Rio Papaloapan.
HABITAT: Lowland streams emptying into Gulf south of Vera Cruz. Among vegetation in ponds and bayous.

178

DESCRIPTION: Rather stocky or stubby in shape; rounded caudal. *Male:* Smaller, usually more intensely hued. Typical poeciliid male breeding apparatus (gonopodium) consisting of modified anal fin. *Female:* Larger, much more robust. "Gravid" spot easily visible on large females shortly prior to birth of young. Body yellow-gold with white belly; dorsal red in both sexes. Variable shaped black spot at caudal peduncle, at times crescent-like; hence the name: Moonfish.

VARIATIONS: Seemingly endless combinations of red, yellow, gold, black, blue, etc. "Wagtail" variety has black caudal, pectorals, ventrals and anal. "Tuxedo" has broad, black lengthwise band on lower sides.

LENGTH: $2\frac{1}{2}$-3 inches; males smaller.

CARE: Excellent, peaceful community fish. Undemanding on water conditions, but soft, acid water to be avoided. In soft water locales, a teaspoon of epsom salts can be added to 5 gallons of water. Planting and aeration desirable.

FEEDING: All fish foods; some vegetation desirable.

BREEDING: Standard livebearer (see *X. helleri*). Prolific. Produces often at 80°F.—27°C.

ORDER: *Atheriniformes*   FAMILY: *Poeciliidae*
SCIENTIFIC NAME: *Xiphophorus maculatus* (Günther).
POPULAR NAME: **Red Tuxedo Platy; Red Tuxedo Moon.**
RANGE: Southern Mexico, Rio Papaloapan.
HABITAT: Lowland streams emptying into Gulf south of Vera Cruz. Ponds and ditches in heavy vegetation.
DESCRIPTION: Stocky, caudal rounded. Shape as with Gold Platy. *Male:* Smaller, with typical male breeding organ. *Female:* Larger; much plumper, more robust. Both sexes blood red or velvet red; sides black. Fins clear or slightly reddish.
VARIATIONS: Fins black as well as sides; also body green, yellow, gold. Many variable combinations.
LENGTH: 2½-3 inches.
CARE: Excellent community fish. Moderately hard, alkaline water best. Temp. 70-82°F.—21-28°C. Planting and aeration desirable.
FEEDING: All fish foods. Feedings should contain some vegetable matter. Best condition if fed several times daily in small amounts.
BREEDING: Heavy females may be isolated in separate aquaria with heavy floating vegetation (*Myriophyllum*, mare's tail, etc.) and fed live food or good substitute. Newborn babies escape into vegetation. Remove mother afterwards. Heavy females should not be moved within a few days of giving birth.

180

Red Tuxedo Platy

181

ORDER: *Atheriniformes*   FAMILY: *Melanotaeniidae*
SCIENTIFIC NAME: *Melanotaenia maccullochi* Ogilby.
POPULAR NAME: **Black-lined Rainbow Fish; Rainbow Fish.**
RANGE: Northern Australia, around Cairns.
HABITAT: Fast-flowing streams.
DESCRIPTION: Body rather deep, compressed and elongate. Two dorsal fins. About 7 dark lengthwise bands on sides, interspaced with pearl-like rows of scales. Caudal reddish to brick red. Dorsal and anal orange with yellow edges, greenish at base. *Male:* Beautiful glowing yellow lateral stripe, especially intense at courtship. *Female:* Less handsome, duller. Abdomen more rounded.
LENGTH: 3-4 inches.
CARE: Excellent, entirely peaceful community fish. Should be kept in schools or groups in roomy, well-aerated aquarium. Water may be neutral or slightly alkaline and moderately soft to moderately hard both for keeping and breeding. Morning sunshine is appreciated and acts as spawning stimulus.
FEEDING: Prefers live food, but will accept almost all high quality foods. Freeze-dried and frozen food as well as flake food are good alternatives.
BREEDING: Several mature pairs placed in an aquarium containing floating bunched plants or artificial spawning plants and positioned to receive morning light will spawn on consecutive mornings

Black-lined Rainbow Fish

for several days at a time. Well-fed parents will produce far more babies than will be eaten, and in about 10 days babies will begin to appear at the surface in search of food. At this point parents can be removed, or may remain. Simply feed the babies in the breeding aquarium on liquid fry food and newly hatched brine shrimp. Some breeders remove the young from the breeding container as they appear. Growth is quite rapid.

ORDER: *Atheriniformes*   FAMILY: *Atherinidae*
SCIENTIFIC NAME: *Telmatherina ladigesi* Ahl.
POPULAR NAME: **Celebes Rainbow Fish.**
RANGE: Celebes, Indonesia.
HABITAT: Flowing streams.
DESCRIPTION: Body elongate, compressed. Two dorsals: first small, black with light rays; second larger. *Male:* Second dorsal with long filaments, the first two rays of second dorsal black, others yellowish. Anal similar; first ray black. Caudal yellowish with black stripe on upper and lower lobes. Back and belly yellow, with over-all blueish look to body. A bright blue to blue-green band on sides from mid-body to caudal. *Female:* Dorsal and anal lacking filaments; duller.
LENGTH: 2½-3 inches.
CARE: Moderately planted aquarium with rather hard, neutral or slightly alkaline water. Aeration and filtration desirable. Best kept in schools of several fish. Regular partial water changes bring out the beautiful hues of this attractive fish. In community, keep with other peaceful fishes of comparable size and requirements.
FEEDING: Live foods; frozen, freeze-dried and best flake and dried foods. Appreciates variety of fare.
BREEDING: Morning sun stimulates spawning on fine-leaved floating plants. Presence of live food prevents egg-eating. Eggs produced daily over long period. Yellowish; hatch in 8-11 days.

Celebes Rainbow Fish

ORDER: *Perciformes*   FAMILY: *Centropomidae*
SCIENTIFIC NAME: *Chanda ranga* (Hamilton-Buchanan).

POPULAR NAME: **Glassfish; Indian Glassfish.**

RANGE: India; Burma; Thailand.

HABITAT: Fresh and brackish water.

DESCRIPTION: Body deep, compressed; quite transparent. Two dorsals. *Male:* Dorsal and anal blue-bordered. *Female:* Duller.

LENGTH: 2-2½ inches.

CARE: Well-planted, dark-bottomed aquarium receiving some natural sunlight if possible. Rather shy, less so if kept in small groups. In community tank, only fishes of similar size and of the most peaceful nature should be included. Water preferably with sea salt or marine salt added, 1 or 2 generous teaspoons to the gallon (most sturdy plants can stand this amount). Although transparency of the flesh does not diminish, the generally very mild amber tone of the flesh seems to deepen with additional salt. It is possibly wise not to exceed, however, a saturation approaching ½ fresh, ½ sea water.

FEEDING: Live food. Daphnia, cyclops, white worms (*Enchytrae*) and for adults the tiniest redworms, mosquito larvae and live brine shrimp (newly hatched is acceptable). Occasionally, Glassfish can be trained to take other than live food, such as frozen brine shrimp or even flake food. The secret seems to be in making the food "look" alive, i.e.

Glassfish ; Indian Glassfish

keep it in motion. Caution must be used not to
overfeed in the attempt to get an adequate amount
of moving food past the fish.

BREEDING: Healthy Glassfish spawn rather readily,
stimulated by fresh morning sunshine entering the
tank. Adhesive eggs are deposited among fine-
leaved plants or on artificial substitute, such as
nylon yarn. Eggs hatch in 24 hours and babies swim
in 3-4 days, until which time parents ignore them.
Young difficult to raise; living food must be in

front of them almost constantly. According to German reports, daphnia in finest sizes is ignored, but fine cyclops are taken apparently owing to difference in swimming action. To author's knowledge, Glassfish have been raised successfully by feeding newly hatched brine shrimp in large amounts; feeding, siphoning left-overs out 6-8 hours later and re-feeding almost immediately.

ORDER: *Perciformes*   FAMILY: *Centrarchidae*
SCIENTIFIC NAME: *Enneacanthus chaetodon* (Baird).
(Sometimes known as *Mesogonistius chaetodon*.)
POPULAR NAME: **Black-banded Sunfish; Banded Sunfish.**
RANGE: New Jersey; Maryland; to South Carolina.
HABITAT: Slow and standing waters; swamps.
DESCRIPTION: Deep-bodied; rather short and laterally compressed. Body silvery grey to olive grey with several dark to black vertical bands, some rather splotchy and broken. Ventrals orange to black; dorsal with front rays strongly spinous, posterior rays soft; connected.
LENGTH: 3-4 inches, often less in aquarium.
CARE: Well-planted, moderately lit aquarium. Rather shy until acclimatized. Large aquarium preferred, aeration beneficial. May be kept with other small Sunfish species. Temperature rather cool, 50-70°F.—10-21°C. Water slightly acid or about neutral.

Black-banded Sunfish

FEEDING: Prefers live food, but will accept frozen brine shrimp, etc. Finely ground beef heart, flake foods occasionally acceptable to individuals.

BREEDING: Male digs depression in sand, coaxes female to deposit spawn which he subsequently guards. Females driven from nest after spawning, and should be removed. Male should be removed when young are free-swimming. Young capable of eating newly hatched brine shrimp as soon as free-swimming.

ORDER: *Perciformes*   FAMILY: *Lobotidae*
SCIENTIFIC NAME: *Datnioides microlepis* Bleeker.
POPULAR NAME: **Siamese Tiger Fish.**
RANGE: Borneo; Sumatra; Cambodia; Thailand.
HABITAT: Swamps, lakes, clear and turbid streams.
DESCRIPTION: Body cream to cream yellowish; 6 jet black vertical bands on sides; one through eye, one broad and one narrow on caudal peduncle, three broad ones on body. Pectoral and caudal clear, ventrals black with light leading edge. Compressed laterally, but well-fleshed. Mouth very large and protruding. Sex differences unknown.
LENGTH: 6-8 inches in aquarium.
CARE: Aggressive; best kept alone or with other fishes able to take care of themselves. If more than one Tiger Fish is to be kept in an aquarium, provide heavy planting of both vertical type plants (such as *Vallisneria*) and floating varieties. Caves should also be available, such as flowerpots split vertically in half, or pieces of large roofing tile. Water not critical; about neutral and not too hard.
FEEDING: Prefers live fishes, but can be trained to accept beef heart and brine shrimp. Larger fish require sizeable chunks of meat or raw fish, or large earthworms (nightcrawlers). Temperature 72-80°F.—22-27°C.
BREEDING: Unknown.

Siamese Tiger Fish

Singapore Angel; Finger Fish; Mono

ORDER: *Perciformes* FAMILY: *Monodactylidae*

SCIENTIFIC NAME: *Monodactylus argenteus* (Linnaeus).

POPULAR NAME: **Singapore Angel; Finger Fish; Mono.**

RANGE: Red Sea; east coast of Africa; Malay Archipelago.

HABITAT: Sea; brackish water; estuaries; sometimes rivers.

DESCRIPTION: Body rather disc-shaped, anal and dorsal giving an angelfish-like impression. Body yellowish silver, becoming more silvery with age and size. Two black vertical bands; one through eye, other from anterior of dorsal, curving downwards, edging anal with black. Caudal yellowish. Ventrals very small.

LENGTH: 5-6 inches in aquarium; seldom more; larger in nature.

CARE: Best kept in brackish or sea water, although does well in moderately hard, somewhat alkaline water, especially in very large aquaria with plenty of swimming space. Less nervous if more than one individual present. Presence of other active, non-shy fishes lessens shyness. *M. argenteus* has a largely undeserved reputation for timidity and delicacy towards handling. Temp. 74-80°F.—23-27°C. is best. May be aggressive, especially toward angelfish and other long-finned, slow-moving fishes.

FEEDING: Heavy feeder. Live, frozen, freeze-dried foods; beef heart. Dried food accepted.

BREEDING: Unsuccessful. One reported spawning indicated cichlid-style egg-placement on stones. Eggs failed to hatch.

193

ORDER: *Perciformes*   FAMILY: *Toxotidae*
SCIENTIFIC NAME: *Toxotes jaculator* (Pallas).
POPULAR NAME: **Archer Fish.**
RANGE: India; Burma; South-east Asia to Philippines and Australia.
HABITAT: Estuaries; river mouths; sometimes ascending rivers into fresh water.
DESCRIPTION: Head rather pointed, mouth large. Body rather deep; silver grey in tone with four distinct cross-bands of black; one through eye, one behind head, one from front of first dorsal and one beneath second dorsal. *T. jaculator* is distinguished from very similar *T. chatareus* by having 4 dorsal spines, while the latter has 5.
LENGTH: 5-6 inches in aquarium; much more in nature.
CARE: Large aquarium with plenty of surface space for swimming. Ideally, an aquarium can be tall, and filled two-thirds full of water with 2 teaspoons or so of rock salt or marine salt to the gallon. Roots, vines, etc. can overhang or come from water, providing excellent "gunnery range" for placing insects or other titbits at which fish can "shoot". Plants may be employed moderately, using hardy species able to withstand the addition of salt. Partial, periodic water changes beneficial. Temperature about 75°F.—24°C.
FEEDING: Live insects of all kinds; meal worms are a practical source of live insects. Worms or

Archer Fish

beetles allowed to crawl on branches, glass, etc. above water line will be "shot down" in an intriguing display of aerial marksmanship. Fish can also be trained to shoot pieces of ground beef heart down, which can be pressed on glass sides of aquarium above water line. Water is expelled in droplet "missiles" by a unique mouth structure powered by a gill-pumping action.

BREEDING: Spawning and sex differences unknown.

Scat; Argus Scat

ORDER: *Perciformes*   FAMILY: *Scatophagidae*
SCIENTIFIC NAME: *Scatophagus argus* (Gmelin).
POPULAR NAME: **Scat; Argus Scat.**
RANGE: Indian Ocean; China to Australia.
HABITAT: Fresh; brackish; sea water. Young enter
backwaters and river, later apparently returning to
sea. Abundant in areas of sewage disposal, etc.
DESCRIPTION: Disc-shaped; flattened. Spinous dor-
sal and soft dorsal almost separate; former heavily

spined. Mouth and head quite small. Body greenish or silver-yellow to brown. Rows of large, blackish spots on sides. Some specimens with red or reddish spots on back and upper head region (incorrectly called *S.* "*rubrifrons*"). Older and larger fish seem to pale somewhat. Sex differences unknown.

LENGTH: 5-6 inches in aquarium; seldom more. Larger in nature.

CARE: Does best in large aquarium. Water should have salt added, preferably sea salt 2-3 teaspoons per gallon. Planting impractical; plants will be eaten. Temp. 70-76°F.—21-24°C. Good community fish with other fishes of similar size and requirements, such as *Monodactylus*. May be kept in fresh water when young, but does best when salt added, progressively increased as fish ages.

FEEDING: Gluttonous; eats almost anything organic. Aquarium specimens sometimes become rather particular about feeding, usually corrected by additional salt. Live foods of all kinds; frozen brine shrimp, quantities of spinach, algae or alfalfa. Fond of pellet-type food; flake food and oatmeal, either cooked or uncooked.

BREEDING: Impractical for most aquarists. Sterba reports one recorded spawning by Rachow in which eggs hatched but fry were subsequently lost. Spawning occurred cichlid-fashion in a crevice of a rock in marine aquarium. Parents undertook brood care.

Leaf Fish

ORDER: *Perciformes*　　　　FAMILY: *Nandidae*

SCIENTIFIC NAME: *Monocirrhus polyacanthus* Heckel.

POPULAR NAME: **Leaf Fish.**

RANGE: Amazon and Rio Negro Basins; Guyana.

HABITAT: Forest streams and pools.

DESCRIPTION: Almost unbelievably leaf-like in appearance. A single barbel on lower jaw (*monocirrhus* = one whisker); head pointed, mouth highly protrusible and capable of engulfing quite sizeable fishes. Brown, sometimes marbled with yellowish green; coloration quite variable according to conditions and surroundings. Posterior dorsal and anal tips clear.

LENGTH: $2\frac{1}{2}$-3 inches.

CARE: Well-planted aquarium preferable, provided with flowerpot or other cave-like situation, especially if spawning is to be attempted. Best kept with own species. Aeration and filtration desirable, since distress due to lack of oxygen or excess carbon dioxide not indicated in normal surface-sucking fashion.

FEEDING: Live fish exclusively.

BREEDING: Spawns in pots or caves rather cichlid-fashion. Male guards eggs.

ORDER: *Perciformes*   FAMILY: *Cichlidae*

SCIENTIFIC NAME: *Aequidens curviceps* (Ahl).

POPULAR NAME: **Flag Cichlid.**

RANGE: Amazon region.

HABITAT: Quiet, slow-flowing waters.

DESCRIPTION: Back brownish green to olive; sides fish-green with delicate yellow and blue. Belly lighter; silvery to light gold. Eye with golden iris, red above. Caudal and anal with light blue or blue-green dots. *Male:* Dorsal and anal longer, more pointed; cheeks with blue streaks. *Female:* Duller; usually smaller, especially if pair spawns frequently. As with other cichlids, the genital papilla, a nipple-like structure produced from vent at breeding time for use in placing and fertilizing eggs, is much larger in the female.

LENGTH: 3-3½ inches.

CARE: An excellent, peaceful cichlid suitable for the community aquarium. Does not destroy plants. Temp. rather warm; 75-82°F.—22-28°C. Water not critical; as long as pH and hardness are not extreme.

FEEDING: Live foods such as daphnia, insect larvae, white worms. Small, bite-size earthworms excellent. Beef heart very good (finely ground). Most foods acceptable.

BREEDING: Spawning site selected, cleaned; parents may eat eggs, but usually spawn again shortly. Care of eggs (see picture) and babies usually exemplary; a beautiful fish to experience.

Flag Cichlid

Blue Acara

ORDER: *Perciformes* FAMILY: *Cichlidae*
SCIENTIFIC NAME: *Aequidens pulcher* (Gill).
POPULAR NAME: **Blue Acara.**
RANGE: Colombia; Panama; Trinidad; Venezuela.
DESCRIPTION: Heavy-bodied; rather compressed.
Grey-green body, adorned with pale neon blue or
green dots over sides. Typical dark ocellus on side
of young and non-breeding fish. Older fish with

electric blue streaks on cheek area, more prominent at breeding. Breeding adults with alternate grey-blue or grey-green vertical bars. *Male:* Longer, more pointed dorsal and anal fins. *Female:* Dorsal and anal less pointed; darker body pattern (not always); often smaller, especially after several spawnings.

LENGTH: 6 inches; breeds at 3-4 inches.

CARE: A sturdy fish, inclined to be aggressive especially at breeding time. Keep in large aquarium with other non-shy, robust species of comparable size and temperament. Only strongest plants can withstand the digging and physical assault of this and other typical cichlids. Rockwork, roots for cover. Prone to excavation; facilitate this by an inch or so of sand or light gravel.

FEEDING: Beef heart, brine shrimp (adult, frozen), small earthworms, pellet foods.

BREEDING: After mutual test of strength, male and female clean spawning site, lay and incubate eggs. Free-swimming babies are supervised, bedded down at night and otherwise cared for. A tremendously interesting beginner's and collector's fish.

Agassiz's Dwarf Cichlid

ORDER: *Perciformes* FAMILY: *Cichlidae*

SCIENTIFIC NAME: *Apistogramma agassizi* (Steindachner).

POPULAR NAME: **Agassiz's Dwarf Cichlid.**

RANGE: Amazon Basin.

DESCRIPTION: Body brownish-yellow to greenish-blue; a dark longitudinal band from mouth to caudal root. *Male:* Dorsal long-based, tip quite long, pointed especially in older fish, reddish at edge and on latter portion. Anal yellowish. Caudal heart-shaped, bordered with blue-grey or grey-green; middle orange with dark. Ventrals quite long; orange and black. *Female:* Smaller; fins shorter. Rather yellowish, much less handsome than male.

LENGTH: 3 inches.

CARE: Well-planted, not too brightly lit aquarium providing plenty of rocks, caves, roots, etc. Water rather soft, slightly acid. Temp. 70-80°F.—21-27°C. Halves of vertically split flower-pots or pieces of roofing tile make excellent cave sites. Rather aggressive.

FEEDING: Prefers live food; mosquito larvae, daphnia, bloodworms, etc. Accepts frozen brine shrimp, finely ground beef heart and highest quality flake foods.

BREEDING: Spawns under rocks or in caves. Female assumes brood care; drives male away. Eggs hatch 2-5 days, babies swim freely 4-6 more days, at which time they can eat tiniest newly hatched shrimp.

Borelli's Dwarf Cichlid

ORDER: *Perciformes*   FAMILY: *Cichlidae*

SCIENTIFIC NAME: *Apistogramma borellii* (Regan).

POPULAR NAME: **Borelli's Dwarf Cichlid.**

RANGE: Mato Grosso, Brazil; Rio Paraguay.

DESCRIPTION: *Male:* Anterior dorsal rays quite long, filament-like; dorsal and anal pointed, greatly elongated; upper and lower lobes of caudal long and pointed; rather lyre-shaped. Dorsal reddish-tipped; dorsal, anal and caudal blueish; caudal and anal with lace-like pattern. Dark lateral band from behind eye to caudal root. Ventrals long. *Female:* Smaller, less handsome, and with shorter fins.

LENGTH: 2½-3 inches.

CARE: Pairs can be kept in small, well-planted aquarium provided with rocks, roots or potential cave sites, such as flower-pots and coconut shell. Temperature preferably warm, rather stable, 74-82°F.—23-28°C. Males aggressive. Moderately soft water, pH neutral to mild acid.

FEEDING: Live food preferred. Frozen brine shrimp, mosquito larvae, etc. Highest quality flake, dry foods.

BREEDING: Spawning takes place under stones, in caves or in cave-like locations. Flowerpots split lengthwise or roofing tile pieces quite useful. After spawning, female assumes brood care, driving male from spawning site. Babies may be moved several times previous to free-swimming. Free-swimming babies take tiniest brine shrimp.

207

ORDER: *Perciformes*   FAMILY: *Cichlidae*

SCIENTIFIC NAME: *Apistogramma reitzigi* Ahl.

POPULAR NAME: **Reitzig's Dwarf Cichlid.**

RANGE: Central Rio Paraguay.

HABITAT: Areas of bank providing rocky caves or roots, etc., suitable for establishing individual territory, at the same time providing good cover.

DESCRIPTION: Sides yellowish-grey; belly, throat bright yellow. Back darker. *Male:* Larger, fins somewhat longer. *Female:* Smaller; darker. Intense yellow during breeding.

LENGTH: 2-2½ inches.

CARE: Suitable in well-planted community providing hiding places, caves, etc. Companion fishes should be small, not boisterous. Moderately soft, near neutral to somewhat acid water. Temperature warm, 75-82°F.—24-28°C. Small, well-planted aquaria housing pairs are ideal.

FEEDING: Preferably live foods such as bloodworms (*Chironomus*), daphnia or mosquito larvae. Frozen brine shrimp, best flake or dried foods supplement diet.

BREEDING: In caves, under rocks or roots, etc. Female becomes bright yellow, drives male away. Male should be removed after spawning. Female assumes brood care.

Reitzig's Dwarf Cichlid

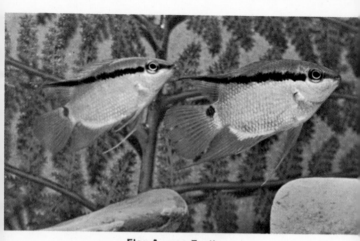

Flag Acara; Festivum

ORDER: *Perciformes* FAMILY: *Cichlidae*
SCIENTIFIC NAME: *Cichlasoma festivum* (Heckel).
POPULAR NAME: **Flag Acara; Festivum.**
RANGE: Amazon Basin; Guyana.
HABITAT: Vegetated shoreline areas.
DESCRIPTION: Greatly elongated ventral fins, reminiscent of angelfish (*Pterophyllum*) with which it is associated in nature. Greatly compressed; anal and dorsal elongated; body brassy above, whitish yellow below. An outstanding black stripe from

corner of mouth through eye to tip of soft dorsal. Light-ringed black ocellus on upper half of caudal peduncle. Fins yellowish with darker lace-like markings. Eye gold or red.

LENGTH: 5 inches, seldom more.

CARE: A shy cichlid requiring good cover. Eats soft-leaved plants. Large species of *Sagittaria* and healthy Amazon swords, plus rockwork and roots are best. Plastic plants may be necessary with some individuals. Large aquarium with other relatively well-tempered cichlids, larger gouramis, etc. A very large, densely planted aquarium containing only angelfish and festivums is a striking display. Temperature 75-85°F.—24-29°C.

FEEDING: Live food; beef heart; occasional vegetable matter. Large dried foods.

BREEDING: A difficult *Cichlasoma*. Spawns cichlid-style on stones, in flowerpots or caves; sometimes on broad-leaved plants. Eggs best removed and hatched artificially. Breeding temperature 80-82°F. —27-28°C.

ORDER: *Perciformes*   FAMILY: *Cichlidae*
SCIENTIFIC NAME: *Cichlasoma octofasciatum* (Regan).
(Incorrectly known as *Cichlasoma biocellatum* Regan.)
POPULAR NAME: **Jack Dempsey Cichlid.**
RANGE: Central America; Southern Mexico; Guatemala; Honduras.
DESCRIPTION: 7 or 8 obscure to distinct dark bands on sides; body grey to grey-brown or black in older fish. Black blotch on third band, connected to obscure lateral band extending to edge of gill cover; similar spot on upper half of caudal peduncle. Lower jaw jutting; brilliant metallic blue. Numerous metallic blue or blue-green spots below eye and on gill cover. Each scale on flanks with blue or blue-green spot, becoming more intense with age. Fins with blue spots alternating with dark on rays, giving beautiful lace-like effect. Dorsal of older fish with fine red or yellow border. Breeding fish intense blue. *Male:* Dorsal and anal pointed. *Female:* Dorsal and anal more rounded.
LENGTH: 6-8 inches in large aquaria.
CARE: Rather pugnacious, especially during breeding. Uproots and tears plants to pieces. Single specimens may sometimes be kept in community with other sturdy fishes. Very old individuals much less pugnacious when kept singly with other species. These are among the most breathtakingly beautiful of fresh-water aquarium fishes.
FEEDING: Earthworms, beef heart, meat or fish pieces.

212

Jack Dempsey Cichlid

BREEDING: After typical cichlid mouth-wrestling, pair selects, cleans spawning site, usually a rock. Female places eggs in rows, which are alternately fertilized by male. Aeration and protection is afforded by fanning until eggs hatch, when they are moved to previously dug depression in sand. May be moved several times. Even after free-swimming, parental protection continues; babies kept in school, bedded down in depression at night. Some degree of parental watchfulness may continue until parents are ready to spawn again. At free-swimming, most cichlid babies can take newly hatched brine shrimp.

Tremendously interesting and rewarding experience.

ORDER: *Perciformes*   FAMILY: *Cichlidae*
SCIENTIFIC NAME: *Hemichromis bimaculatus* Gill.
POPULAR NAME: **Jewel Fish; Jewel Cichlid.**
RANGE: Congo; Niger; Nile; very common in tropical Africa.
DESCRIPTION: At breeding season, undoubtedly one of the most beautiful of tropical fishes. Back greenish with brown to orange overtone; becoming brilliant red to red orange at breeding. Iridescent blueish flecks on body and fins. Black spot on opercular cover; another on side (*bimaculatus* = two spots). Female often takes on coloration during spawning.
LENGTH: 5-6 inches.
CARE: Extremely pugnacious when adult. Can be kept only with other ill-tempered and large fishes in the largest aquaria. When this is possible (not always) the beautiful red, although not as intense as during breeding, is almost constantly retained. After one spawning, pairs must usually be isolated. A "digger".

Jewel Fish; Jewel Cichlid

FEEDING: Earthworms; beef heart; pellet foods. Most foods acceptable.

BREEDING: Once a pair has mated, a beautiful display of site-cleaning and parental care occurs. Spawns are large. Babies are easily started and raised on newly hatched brine shrimp. Breeding temperature 80-82°F.—27-28°C.

Fuelleborn's Cichlid

ORDER: *Perciformes*   FAMILY: *Cichlidae*

SCIENTIFIC NAME: *Labeotropheus fuelleborni* Ahl.

POPULAR NAME: **Fuelleborn's Cichlid.**

RANGE: Lake Malawi (formerly Lake Nyasa), Africa.

HABITAT: Rocky shores.

DESCRIPTION: *Male:* Body blue with 10 or 12 darker vertical bars on sides. Mouth underslung; adapted for algal grazing. Posterior of dorsal and anal with orange spots. Anal fin with typical cichlid "egg-spots". *Female:* Similar, or mottled black with gold.

LENGTH: 5-6 inches.

CARE: Well-lighted, roomy aquarium with plenty of rocks, roots, etc. May be kept with other cichlids of similar size and requirements. Water should be rather hard and alkaline. A teaspoon or so of sea salt or rock salt per gallon is beneficial. Aquarium may be planted with sturdy, well-anchored plants. Temp. warm, 75-82°F.—24-28°C. Well-filtered, aerated aquarium preferred.

FEEDING: Accepts most foods, especially live foods, frozen brine shrimp, etc. Largely vegetarian in nature, diet should include large quantities of vegetable matter: oatmeal, spinach, alfalfa pellets. Heavy feeder.

BREEDING: Mouth-brooder. Female assumes oral incubation duties.

ORDER: *Perciformes*   FAMILY: *Cichlidae*

SCIENTIFIC NAME: *Labeotropheus trewavasae* Fryer.

POPULAR NAME: **Red-top Cichlid.**

RANGE: Lake Malawi (formerly Lake Nyasa), Africa.

HABITAT: Rocky shores.

DESCRIPTION: Body rather elongate, somewhat compressed but well-fleshed. *Male:* Body blue with 10 or 12 darker vertical bars on sides; dorsal red. Upper lip overhanging, fleshy in appearance. Whitish stripe on forehead between eyes. *Female:* May be mottled, black, orange, yellow. Also with overhanging, flesh-like lip.

LENGTH: 5-6 inches.

CARE: Preferably large aquarium. Plenty of rocks, roots and other cover; males quite aggressive. Water rather hard and alkaline. A teaspoon or two of salt per gallon is appreciated by this and other "mbunas". Temp. rather warm, 75-82°F.—24-28°C. Aeration beneficial. Aquarium should be brightly lighted to promote natural algal growth if possible.

FEEDING: Largely vegetarian, prefers algae. Most fish foods acceptable. Most will accept boiled oatmeal, cooked spinach, alfalfa pellets, etc., as well as ground beef heart, frozen brine shrimp, etc. Heavy feeder.

BREEDING: Not difficult, although not extremely prolific. Mouth-brooder, female incubating fry. Male may occasionally incubate a few fry.

Red-top Cichlid

ORDER: *Perciformes*   FAMILY: *Cichlidae*

SCIENTIFIC NAME: *Pelmatochromis pulcher* Boulenger.

POPULAR NAME: **"Kribensis"**—but this is a mis-nomer, for it is the name of another fish (*P. kribensis*).

RANGE: West Africa; Niger delta.

DESCRIPTION: Upper side dark greenish brown to dull brown; dark stripe on side from opercular to caudal; brassy gold to greyish above and below. Belly pink to bright red. Dorsal red-edged. *Male:* Dorsal prolonged, pointed at end. Caudal with reddish upper edge, with spots on upper portion. *Female:* Smaller, much heavier-bodied; belly red.

LENGTH: 3-4 inches.

CARE: Heavily planted, moderately lighted aquarium providing plenty of rocks, cave sites, etc. Flowerpots, either split vertically or notched at rim to provide entrance, make excellent caves. Best kept with own kind. Water not too hard, about neutral or slightly acid. A teaspoon or so of sea salt or rock salt per gallon is beneficial. A digger, especially under rocks and other objects. Temperature 75-80°F.—24-27°C.

FEEDING: Prefers live food or frozen brine shrimp, other frozen foods. Small earthworms are relished by fish large enough to eat them. Will accept finely ground beef heart, flake foods.

BREEDING: Cave-spawner. Flowerpot, beneath rock or other cave site is well excavated and cleaned for spawning site. After spawning, male is dismissed and should be removed. Female may be left for brood care, but some breeders remove her after young are free-swimming.

Golden Cichlid

ORDER: *Perciformes*   FAMILY: *Cichlidae*
SCIENTIFIC NAME: *Pseudotropheus auratus* (Boulenger).
POPULAR NAME: **Golden Cichlid; Golden Pseudotropheus.**
RANGE: Lake Malawi (formerly Lake Nyasa), Africa.
HABITAT: Rocky shores, bays.
DESCRIPTION: Three longitudinal stripes, one from forehead through eye to caudal fin, one above this

and parallel to it, the third along the dorsal fin. In mature *males* these are electric blue on a nearly black ground. In *females* and *young* the stripes are black, edged with blue, on a gold background. When alarmed, males can change to female coloration and back again when fear has passed. Male often has "egg-spots" on anal fin.

LENGTH: About 6 inches; sometimes less.

CARE: Well-lighted aquarium providing plenty of cover, such as caves, rocks, roots, etc. May be kept with other cichlids of similar size and requirements. Water rather hard and alkaline; 1 or 2 teaspoons of rock salt or marine salt per gallon beneficial. Temp. warm, 75-82°F.—24-28°C. Heavy aeration and filtration desirable to ensure water clarity. Large aquarium if possible, since males are aggressive.

FEEDING: Live, frozen and .freeze-dried foods usually accepted eagerly. Also ground beef heart. Largely vegetarian in nature. Lettuce, spinach, carrot or celery tops, as well as cooked oatmeal. As with many cichlids, competition broadens range of appetite.

BREEDING: Mouth-brooder; female assuming brood care. Not difficult, although not prolific. Upon release by mother, babies can take newly hatched brine shrimp.

ORDER: *Perciformes*　　　　　　FAMILY: *Cichlidae*

SCIENTIFIC NAME: *Pseudotropheus elongatus.*

POPULAR NAME: **Elongate Mbuna** (pronounced um-BU-na).

RANGE: Lake Malawi (formerly Lake Nyasa), Africa.

HABITAT: Rocky shores.

DESCRIPTION: *Male:* Head black to blueish black, body deep blue or purple; about 8 black vertical bars some of which are more or less distinct at various times. Lighter areas rather ice-blue or powder blue during breeding; fins edged in ice-blue. This is a long, slender-bodied cichlid. *Female:* Much lighter, duller. Rather light purple or greyish purple, darkening somewhat at spawning, dorsal lightening in soft rays. Both sexes may exhibit "egg-spots" on anal, but male's larger and more distinct.

LENGTH: 5 inches.

CARE: Large aquarium receiving plenty of light. Numerous rocks, caves in which to hide and under which to dig. Hard, alkaline water, pH 7.6 to 8.6 is ideal. Addition of sea salt or rock salt recommended; 2-3 teaspoons per gallon is not too much. Very aggressive; single pairs must be separated although several fish may work in reasonable harmony if enough cover is available, since bullying will not be excessively concentrated on an individual. Temp. 72-80°F.—22-27°C.

FEEDING: Brine shrimp, beef heart, flake foods and

Elongate Mbuna

live foods eaten with relish. As with other Mbunas vegetation is a large component of the natural diet. Should be offered spinach, lettuce, celery tops, carrot tops or alfalfa pellets.

BREEDING: Mouth-brooder. Female assumes brood care and may be removed as gently as possible when it is noticed that she is carrying eggs in her mouth. Babies may eat brine shrimp immediately upon becoming free-swimming.

225

ORDER: *Perciformes*   FAMILY: *Cichlidae*
SCIENTIFIC NAME: *Pterophyllum scalare* (Lichtenstein).
POPULAR NAME: **Angelfish; Scalare.**
RANGE: Amazon.
HABITAT: Vegetated stretches of slow-moving water.
DESCRIPTION: Similar to the more common *P. eimekei*. The body is much deeper in *P. eimekei*, and *P. scalare* is more prominently banded. Four black vertical bands through eye, shoulder, dorsal and caudal peduncle with three less distinct bands between. Bright silver with an olive or greenish sheen. *Male:* Profile from breast through anal straighter than in female; breeding tube less prominent at breeding. *Female:* Junction of belly and anal fin slightly more indented; ovipositor at spawning much heavier, more prominent.
LENGTH: 5 inches.
CARE: Well-planted, warm aquarium; preferably only with other angelfish, discus or festivum. A good breeding pair best kept by themselves. Temp. 75-82°F.—24-28°C. Large aquarium.
FEEDING: Live foods, especially baby fishes, mosquito larvae. Frozen brine shrimp good, but water should frequently be partially changed. Beef heart.
BREEDING: Spawns cichlid-style on broad plant leaves, slate or aquarium glass; also other vertical

Angelfish; Scalare

sites. In quiet location parents may raise babies; often they are eaten, however. Safer is to remove eggs and hatch artificially in aerated bare container at 80°F.—27°C.

ORDER: *Perciformes*   FAMILY: *Cichlidae*
SCIENTIFIC NAME: *Symphysodon discus* Heckel.
POPULAR NAME: **Discus; "Common" Discus.**
RANGE: Amazon; Rio Negro; Rio Cupai, and other tributaries, South America.
HABITAT: Root-tangled, vegetated bank areas.
DESCRIPTION: Disc-shaped; mouth quite small; mouth region slightly forward-pointed. Sides reddish brown to golden brown; on adult specimens numerous electric blue, horizontal-angled streaks projecting backwards along body from head region. Nine vertical bars, three of which are distinct. These darkish or blue (according to Schultz) bars are numbers 1, 5 and 9, with others a rather indistinct tan. At a glance, *S. discus* is made distinctly noticeable by its well defined, midside vertical band. Of the two legitimate discus (*Symphysodon*) species and two additional (and doubtful) sub-species, *S. discus* has a bar through the eye, another at midside, and another at the caudal base; others are much less intense. The other species *S. aequifasciata*, has three varieties; the so-called "brown", "green" and "blue" versions. On the latter three varieties the nine vertical bars are almost equally distinct or indistinct as the case might be. There are numerous photographic misrepresentations in publication.
LENGTH: 6 inches in the aquarium.
CARE: Large, well-aerated and filtered aquarium, not too heavily planted since this may induce

Discus; "Common" Discus

shyness. Presence of angelfish sometimes stimulates competitive instinct, improving appetite and reducing shyness. Water moderately soft, neutral to rather acid. *Most important* is to make frequent partial water changes and to keep aquarium clean. Temp. 72-80°F.—22-27°C.

FEEDING: Frozen brine shrimp, small earthworms, beef heart. Avoid tubifex and other potentially contaminated foods. To these are traceable the unusual discus maladies.

BREEDING: Spawn on plant leaves or slate similar to

229

angelfish. An expensive, specialized fish which requires special treatment. First food of babies is taken from parents' sides. Specialized literature recommended.

ORDER: *Perciformes*   FAMILY: *Gobiidae*

SCIENTIFIC NAME: *Brachygobius nunus* (Hamilton-Buchanan). (Incorrectly "*B. xanthozonus*", distinguished by all-black anal fin, higher scale count on lateral series.)

POPULAR NAME: **Bumblebee Fish; Bumblebee Goby.**

RANGE: Thailand; Malay Peninsula; Greater Sunda Islands, Indonesia; India; Burma.

HABITAT: Brackish, fresh water; rivers and river mouths.

DESCRIPTION: Four brown to black vertical bands, yellow to golden yellow interspaces; broadest in pectoral region; third band passing through posterior portion of anal, anterior portion light. Face grey. Several similar species, of which *B. nunus* is most common.

LENGTH: $1\frac{1}{2}$-$1\frac{3}{4}$ inches.

CARE: Aquarium with small, non-aggressive species. Salt in the amount of 2 teaspoons or more per gallon should be added for best conditions. Finnipper; not to be kept with long-finned, slow-moving fishes. Ideal for separate aquarium provided with half flower-pot or roofing tile used as cave.

Bumblebee Fish; Bumblebee Goby

FEEDING: Live food almost indispensable. Some specimens will accept frozen brine shrimp.
BREEDING: Breeding temp. 80°F.—27°C. Heavy feedings of live foods, preferably varied. Spawning stimulated by water changes. Spawn in flowerpots, caves or under stones; spawn guarded by male parent; hatch in 4-5 days. Difficult to breed successfully.

231

ORDER: *Perciformes*   FAMILY: *Anabantidae*

SCIENTIFIC NAME: *Betta splendens* Regan.

POPULAR NAME: **Siamese Fighting Fish; Betta.**

RANGE: Southeast Asia; Malay Peninsula; Thailand.

HABITAT: Rice fields; ditches; slow-flowing waterways.

DESCRIPTION: *Male:* Dorsal, anal and caudal fins long and flowing; many brilliant variations and combinations. Ventrals blood red; quite long. *Female:* Same, less brilliant; short fins. This is the legendary "fighting fish".

VARIATIONS: Solid red, blue, green, black; light (cream-pink) body with fins to match; albino (rare).

LENGTH: $2\frac{1}{2}$ inches.

CARE: Males must be kept individually. Can be kept in certain community situations with non-aggressive fishes. Females can ordinarily be kept together. Temp. 70-82°F.—21-28°C. Aeration unnecessary because of accessory air-breathing organ. Can be kept in individual pint containers, although frequent cleaning necessary for best condition.

FEEDING: Live, frozen and freeze-dried brine shrimp, tubifex, mosquito larvae, etc. Highest quality flake and dried foods.

BREEDING: Male builds bubble nest; drives female beneath; wraps her in an embrace during which eggs are expelled and fertilized. Female may or

232

Siamese Fighting Fish; Betta

may not help deposit eggs in nest. Remove female; male cares for young until free-swimming, after which he should be removed. Temperature 80-82°F.—27-28°C. First food: infusoria.

Honey Gourami

ORDER: *Perciformes*   FAMILY: *Anabantidae*
SCIENTIFIC NAME: *Colisa chuna* (Hamilton-Buchanan).
POPULAR NAME: **Honey Gourami.**
RANGE: Northeastern India and Assam.
HABITAT: Rivers, weedy areas.
DESCRIPTION: *Male:* A more or less distinct lateral band from eye to lower half of caudal base; dorsal, yellow gold; throat and belly grey-brown to darker, lower front portion of anal dark; sides

honey-toned, tan-gold; ventrals long and thread-like, yellow gold. *Female:* Drab; slightly smaller and heavier in the abdomen. Lateral band also present. Dull greenish tan.

LENGTH: 2 inches or less.

CARE: Temp. rather warm, 75-82°F.—24-28°C. Well-planted aquarium with other small, non-aggressive fishes. As with *C. lalia*, rather shy, becoming less so in the presence of non-shy fishes, especially if cover is available in the form of floating plants, root systems or long-stemmed plants. As with other anabantids, no aeration is required because of their air-breathing capability, although filtration helps keep water clear in any aquarium, obviously a desirable idea.

FEEDING: Live, freeze-dried and frozen foods. Mosquito larvae and bloodworms (*Chironomus*) excellent. High quality flake and dried foods.

BREEDING: Male builds bubble nest similar to *C. lalia*, incorporating perhaps less vegetation. Not difficult. Breeding males less aggressive toward female than *C. lalia*. Babies need quantities of infusoria.

Dwarf Gourami

ORDER: *Perciformes*   FAMILY: *Anabantidae*
SCIENTIFIC NAME: *Colisa lalia* (Hamilton-Buchanan).
POPULAR NAME: **Dwarf Gourami.**
RANGE: India; Bengal; Assam.
HABITAT: Rivers such as Ganges and Jumna, India.
DESCRIPTION: Body greatly compressed and deep, almost oval-shaped. Long, thread-like ventrals

which serve as "feelers". *Male:* Vertically banded with red and blue to blue-green; a rather lace-like, delicate pattern of alternating scale colorations forms the bars; dorsal, caudal and rearward half of anal, scarlet; throat and head, as well as belly, brilliant neon green. Ventrals red-orange. *Female:* Much duller, rounded dorsal and anal.

LENGTH: 2½ inches. Female usually somewhat smaller.

CARE: Well-planted aquarium with other small and harmless fishes. Rather timid, but adequate plant cover and other non-shy fishes help overcome this. Some floating plants are beneficial in promoting a feeling of security. Temp. 75-82°F.—22-28°C.

FEEDING: All high quality foods. Insect larvae, such as mosquito or *Chironomus*, are excellent. Frozen and freeze-dried brine shrimp, etc., also very good.

BREEDING: 15-gallon aquarium, since smaller causes more difficulty feeding babies. Male builds elaborate nest reinforced with plant bits, cares for non-swimming young. Temperature stability important in successfully raising young. Breeding temperature 82°F.—28°C. Breeding males are among most beautiful of aquarium fishes.

Paradise Fish

ORDER: *Perciformes* FAMILY: *Anabantidae*
SCIENTIFIC NAME: *Macropodus opercularis* (Linnaeus).
POPULAR NAME: **Paradise Fish.**
RANGE: China; Korea; Southeast Asia.
HABITAT: Ditches; backwaters; slow-flowing streams; rice fields.
DESCRIPTION: *Male:* Outstandingly beautiful. Caudal long, bright red with upper and lower lobes greatly extended; sides adorned with alternate blue

to blue-green vertical bars; ventrals red; anal and dorsal usually red-brown with dark and pale spots, sometimes blue; edges white. *Female:* Smaller and less handsome. Fins smaller.

VARIATIONS: Albino; fin and body variations in tones and placements of reds, blues and greens.

LENGTH: To 4 inches. Mature much smaller.

CARE: Pugnacious. Can be maintained together if plenty of cover available. Suitable companions are medium-sized cichlids, Silver Dollars (*Metynnis*, etc.) and other hardy species of comparable size. Temp. 50-80°F.—10-27°C., even lower if not for too long. Easily maintained. Air-breather; no aeration required.

FEEDING: All fish foods. Flake and live or frozen foods appreciated.

BREEDING: Well-fed pair will spawn easily by simply raising temp. to 78-80°F.—26-27°C. Male builds bubble nest, cares for spawn and newly hatched young. Remove female after spawning; male, when babies are free-swimming. First food: infusoria or "green water".

Chocolate Gourami

ORDER: *Perciformes* FAMILY: *Anabantidae*
SCIENTIFIC NAME: *Sphaerichthys osphronemoides* Canestrini.

POPULAR NAME: **Chocolate Gourami.**

RANGE: Malay Peninsula; Sumatra.

HABITAT: Pools and ditches.

DESCRIPTION: Chocolate to red-brown on body, yellow-tan to whitish transverse bars variably placed on body. Fins chocolate to red-brown, ventrals elongated; anal dark-bordered, outlined in fine, narrow light edge. Young with light horizontal band. *Male:* More handsome, more sharply pointed dorsal. *Female:* More robust.

LENGTH: 2½ inches.

CARE: Rather delicate. Well-planted aquarium receiving moderate light; soft, acid water. Temperature 75-85°F.—26-29°C.

FEEDING: Live food primarily. Mosquito larvae; bloodworms; live brine shrimp.

BREEDING: Difficult. A mouth-breeder. Spawns small and young rather difficult to raise; slow growing. Breeding temperature 82°F.—28°C.

ORDER: *Perciformes*   FAMILY: *Anabantidae*
SCIENTIFIC NAME: *Trichogaster leeri* (Bleeker).
POPULAR NAME: **Pearl Gourami; Mosaic Gourami.**
RANGE: Malay Peninsula; Thailand; Sumatra; Borneo.
HABITAT: Ditches, backwaters, etc.
DESCRIPTION: Body elongate, laterally compressed; ventrals extremely long, thread-like, used as "feelers". A dark, longitudinal band from caudal through eye. Back brownish yellow or green, sides brown to cream, numerous round, pearl-like spots adorning body and fins. *Male:* Dorsal pointed; breeding males red-breasted; anal much larger than female, eventually with fin-rays separating into lace-like filaments. Older breeding males breathtakingly beautiful. *Female:* Smaller, plainer, rounded dorsal.
LENGTH: 5 inches; female somewhat less.
CARE: Excellent in well-planted community aquarium. Ordinarily quite peaceful; males sometimes aggressive toward each other. Temperature warm, 75-85°F.—24-29°C. Keep with other peaceful species.
FEEDING: Most high quality foods. Insect larvae excellent. Frozen, freeze-dried, flake foods.
BREEDING: Largest fish best breeders. Male builds large bubble nest, cares for young until they are

Pearl Gourami; Mosaic Gourami

free-swimming. Large breeding aquarium recommended. Remove female after spawning, male when babies are free-swimming. First food: infusoria, "green water".

ORDER: *Perciformes*   FAMILY: *Anabantidae*
SCIENTIFIC NAME: *Trichogaster trichopterus* (Pallas).
POPULAR NAME: **Blue Gourami; Three-spot Gourami; Opaline** or **Cosby Gourami** (last variety is the one pictured here).
RANGE: Malaysia; Thailand; Southeast Asia; Greater Sunda Islands, Indonesia; *T. trichopterus sumatranus* from Sumatra.
HABITAT: Canals; rivers; ditches.
DESCRIPTION: Pale, almost silvery blue with more or less darker blue mottling, especially at breeding. Long, thread-like ventrals used as "feelers". *Male:* Dorsal longer and pointed (male pictured). Fins with light spots. *Female:* Similar to male; shorter, rounded dorsal, heavier abdomen.
VARIETIES: Milk-chocolate; heavy dark blue marbling without distinct spot under dorsal and at caudal base. Pale blue, pale brown with distinct black caudal and sub-dorsal spots ("three-spot", counting eye as one spot).
LENGTH: 5-6 inches.
CARE: Well-planted aquarium with other medium-sized fishes. Quite hardy and reasonably peaceful. Males rather aggressive toward females at breeding time.
FEEDING: Almost any good quality food. Live food, of course, is especially appreciated.
BREEDING: An excellent "first egg-layer". Male builds massive bubble nest, wraps female, deposits

Cosby Gourami

eggs in nest and cares for non-swimming babies. Temp. 80-82°F.—27-28°C. 10-15 gallon aquarium. Eggs hatch in 24-48 hours. Remove male, feed infusoria or substitute.

ORDER: *Perciformes*   FAMILY: *Anabantidae*

SCIENTIFIC NAME: *Trichopsis pumilus* (Arnold).

POPULAR NAME: **Green Croaking Gourami.**

The name is due to an audible croaking or purring sound sometimes produced by male fish during quarrels or courtship.

RANGE: Malay Peninsula; Thailand; South Vietnam; India; Sumatra.

HABITAT: Slow-moving small streams; ditches.

DESCRIPTION: Rather "Betta-shaped" body. Ventrals elongated, first ray strong, stiffly feeler-like. Caudal rounded or bluntly pointed. Back dark olive to olive-brown. Belly greenish to greenish-white; over-all with pearly iridescence. Dorsal rather long, with reddish leading edge; greenish to yellow-green or sea-mist-green. Ventrals yellow to whitish. *Male:* More slender; brighter. *Female:* Duller; belly more obviously rounded when well-conditioned, especially when viewed from beneath through clear container.

LENGTH: 1½ inches.

CARE: Rather shy, best in well-planted aquarium. May be kept with other non-aggressive, un-boisterous fishes, or pairs may be kept in small aquaria of their own. Floating plants are appreciated and are important in breeding procedure. Water moderately soft, neutral or slightly acid, preferably warm; 75-80°F.—24-27°C. Do not keep with over-active fishes which might intimidate

Green Croaking Gourami

them. Males may be quarrelsome with each other, but little harm is done.

FEEDING: Small live food preferred; also frozen or freeze-dried as well as highest quality prepared food.

BREEDING: Male builds small bubble nest usually beneath or among floating plants. After completion, female is wrapped in an embrace. Eggs are expelled, placed in nest by male, after which they are guarded by male until free-swimming. After spawning, female ignores eggs. Eggs, numbering perhaps 40-50, hatch in 1-2 days. Free-swimming babies take infusoria, liquid fry food; later newly hatched brine shrimp. Large aquarium unnecessary for either keeping or breeding this interesting, attractive species.

ORDER: *Tetraodontiformes*   FAMILY: *Tetraodontidae*
SCIENTIFIC NAME: *Tetraodon fluviatilis* Hamilton-Buchanan.
POPULAR NAME: **Green Puffer; Puffer.**
RANGE: India; Burma; Thailand; Malaysia; Philippines.
HABITAT: Estuaries, seas and fresh water, such as large rivers.
DESCRIPTION: Almost egg-shaped, usually with dermal spines which become more noticeable when fish is puffed full of air, at which time it is quite globe-shaped. Upper half bright, somewhat brassy yellowish-green with numerous black or dark spots over sides and back. Pattern variable. Belly white, greyish in older fish. Very active; seldom still.
LENGTH: 5 inches or less in aquarium; usually less.
CARE: Best kept in aquarium with other Puffers or other brackish water species such as Scats and Monos. *T. fluviatilis* may be kept in pure fresh water, but water should be somewhat hard and

Green Puffer; Puffer

alkaline. Do not keep with long-finned or slow-moving fishes; a fin-nipper.

FEEDING: Eats anything. All fish foods, especially live and frozen foods. Extremely fond of snails, especially red ramshorns. Small redworms and freeze-dried tubifex excellent conditioners.

BREEDING: Difficult. Spawn on rocks, etc. Male actually protects spawn by covering with his body, cares for young after hatching.

Congo Puffer; Leopard Puffer

ORDER: *Tetraodontiformes*   FAMILY: *Tetraodontidae*
SCIENTIFIC NAME: *Tetraodon schoutedeni* Pellegrin.
POPULAR NAME: **Congo Puffer; Leopard Puffer.**
RANGE: Lower Congo; Stanley Pool, Africa.
HABITAT: Strictly fresh water.
DESCRIPTION: Deflated body rather oval or egg-shaped, rather similar to *T. fluviatilis*. Eye iridescent reddish; body light yellow-green, darker on dorsal surface, lighter on belly. Numerous black roundish spots of different sizes over sides and back. *Male:* Smaller. *Female:* Larger, somewhat more robust.
LENGTH: 3-3½ inches; males smaller.
CARE: Peaceful; may be kept in community aquarium with other fishes of comparable size. Nibbles plants. May be periodically aggressive toward own kind. Temperature 72-80°F.—22-27°C.
FEEDING: Live foods, especially small worms such as white worms (*Enchytrae*) and tubifex. Will accept freeze-dried tubifex readily as well as frozen brine shrimp. Fond of crushed snails, but less efficient at cracking their shells than some tetraodontids.
BREEDING: Difficult, although possible. Pair circle each other in courtship, after which eggs are deposited, fertilized, on rocks or plants. Male assumes brood-care, covering eggs with body. Newly hatched young moved to trench-like depression until free-swimming. Free-swimming young take infusoria.

251

SCIENTIFIC NAME INDEX

INDEX